"Rich in story, here is a work that creatively unfolds the heart of faith as confidence in God, with helpful implications for matters of doubt, prayer and guidance."

Bruce Demarest, professor of theology and spiritual formation, Denver Seminary, Denver, Colorado

"*In Search of a Confident Faith* is a delightful exploration of developing one's trust in an ever-faithful God. Moreland and Issler offer candid glimpses into their personal faith walk and their struggle to find balance between 'head' faith and 'heart' faith. This book provides an important contribution toward understanding the development of personal confident faith in those traditions that tend to dichotomize head and heart in all religious matters, giving permission to both traditions to embrace the other. In addition to an eloquent articulation of faith which integrates intellect and affection, Issler and Moreland offer the reader practical suggestions for personal growth in God-confidence. A must-read for all those concerned with Christian spiritual formation!"

Lisa Milligan Long, assistant professor of Christian formation, Lee University, Cleveland, Tennessee

"Moreland and Issler demonstrate how critical thinking and heartfelt religion go hand in hand, while encouraging God-confidence in the lives of Christians. Drawing upon their personal experiences as well as a lifetime of commitment to higher education, the authors model a spiritual balance too often neglected in understanding the dynamic relationship between Christian faith, hope and love."

Don Thorsen, professor of theology and chair of advanced studies, Haggard Graduate School of Theology, Azusa Pacific University

"Many books focus on either intellectual or emotional barriers to faith. What makes this one unique is the profound way it combines both. In addition to identifying and helping us remove barriers, it also includes many practical, positive strategies for building our God-confidence. As I read it, I found myself not only being informed but also being inspired. Often I found myself praying, 'Lord, increase my faith.' I am confident you will too."

Stephen A. Seamands, professor of Christian doctrine, Asbury Theological Seminary

"The volume is an invitation from ~~Father~~ ⌐ hildren to live by faith, which the authors (~~. J. P. Moreland~~ and Klaus Issler, not only edible witnesses' of God's supernatural act: ed treatment in guiding believers to grow i their beliefs and daily practices."

Linda Pyun, associate dean (...ians, The King's College, Los Angeles

"This book is warmly personal, readable, engaging and edifying, and will challenge readers spiritually as well as intellectually. The insights and testimonies deeply encouraged my own faith, provoking me to remember in a new way God's acts of kindness in my own life."

Craig Keener, professor of New Testament, Palmer Theological Seminary

"We live in a world dominated by a kind of practical atheism. Some of us may vaguely believe in God or even trust Christ as our Savior, but still think and act as if God was not really present. We need a robust faith that sees beyond the moment and brings forth lives lived in the conscious presence of a God who is engaged with the world. J. P. Moreland and Klaus Issler call this God-confidence. Their counsel on how to move toward such a faith is biblically based, theologically and philosophically sound, and experientially confirmed. This is a book to grow on."

James W. Sire, author of *The Universe Next Door* and coauthor with Carl Peraino of *Deepest Differences: A Christian-Atheist Dialogue*

in search
of a
confident
F A I T H

OVERCOMING BARRIERS
TO TRUSTING IN GOD

J. P. MORELAND AND KLAUS ISSLER

IVP Books

An imprint of InterVarsity Press
Downers Grove, Illinois

Inter-Varsity Press

Nottingham, England

InterVarsity Press, USA
P.O. Box 1400, Downers Grove, IL 60515-1426, USA
World Wide Web: www.ivpress.com
Email: email@ivpress.com

Inter-Varsity Press, England
Norton Street, Nottingham NG7 3HR, England
Website: www.ivpbooks.com
Email: ivp@ivpbooks.com

©2008 by J. P. Moreland and Klaus Issler

InterVarsity Press®, USA, is the book-publishing division of InterVarsity Christian Fellowship/USA®, a student movement active on campus at hundreds of universities, colleges and schools of nursing in the United States of America, and a member movement of the International Fellowship of Evangelical Students. For information about local and regional activities, write Public Relations Dept., InterVarsity Christian Fellowship/USA, 6400 Schroeder Rd., P.O. Box 7895, Madison, WI 53707-7895, or visit the IVCF website at <www.intervarsity.org>.

Inter-Varsity Press, England, is closely linked with the Universities and Colleges Christian Fellowship, a student movement connecting Christian Unions in universities and colleges throughout Great Britain, and a member movement of the International Fellowship of Evangelical Students. Website: www.uccf.org.uk.

All Scripture quotations, unless otherwise indicated, are taken from the Holy Bible, New International Version®. NIV®. Copyright © 1973, 1978, 1984 by International Bible Society. Used by permission of Zondervan Publishing House. Distributed in the U.K. by permission of Hodder and Stoughton Ltd. All rights reserved. "NIV" is a registered trademark of International Bible Society. UK trademark number 1448790.

Design: Janelle Rebel
Images: plainpicture/Morla, D.

USA ISBN 978-0-8308-3428-0
UK ISBN 978-1-84474-327-8

Printed in the United States of America ∞

 InterVarsity Press is committed to protecting the environment and to the responsible use of natural resources. As a member of Green Press Initiative we use recycled paper whenever possible. To learn more about the Green Press Initiative, visit <www.greenpressinitiative.org>.

Library of Congress Cataloging-in-Publication Data

Moreland, James Porter, 1948-
  In search of a confident faith: overcoming barriers to trusting in
  God / by J. P. Moreland and Klaus Issler.
     p. cm.
  Includes bibliographical references.
  ISBN 978-0-8308-3428-0 (pbk.: alk. paper)
  1. Faith. 2. Trust in God. I. Issler, Klaus Dieter. II. Title.
  BV4637.M58 2008
  234'.23—dc22

                                                          2008017361

P   24 23 22 21 20 19 18 17 16 15 14 13 12 11 10 9 8 7 6 5 4 3 2
Y   28 27 26 25 24 23 22 21 20 19 18 17 16 15 14 13 12 11 10 09 08

To our precious grandchildren

Katherine Anya Issler (Klaus)

Taylor May Brady and Jonah Carlos Delgado (J. P.)

"Their angels in heaven always see the face

of my Father in heaven."

JESUS OF NAZARETH (MATTHEW 18:10)

CONTENTS

PREFACE

Faith has a public relations problem. It has a hollow ring to it, and it's associated with a lot of really bad, harmful ideas. It no longer carries the rich and deep connotation one finds in the Bible, and very few people know what it really means. Interestingly and sometimes sadly, words change their meaning over time. *Large* used to mean, well, large! Now if you want a large meal, you have to ask for it to be super-sized! If you say *large* you will be misunderstood, and if you want people to understand the meaning of *large* as it used to be understood, you must select a new word.

This shift in the meaning of *large* is amusing, but the change in the meaning of other words, such as *love* or *marriage*, is no laughing matter. The same must be said for *faith*. In fact, in this book, we shall discuss this change in the meaning of *faith*, and, while the word is still biblical, we will suggest in the pages to follow that we should use the term *God-confidence* to convey the biblical meaning of *faith* more often than using *faith* itself. We do not want to completely set aside the word *faith*. But the really important thing for Christians is to recapture and promote the biblical meaning of *faith*, not the word itself, so we shall suggest that *God-confidence* be used regularly when *faith* is meant in speech or writing.

We shall also show why Christians should speak in the public arena by employing cognitive and not simply faith language when referring to Christianity. We ought to talk about the *knowledge* of God—about the Bible as a source of *knowledge* of God, values and wisdom—and not merely say we believe in the Bible or have faith in God. If we call Christianity "the faith" or say "our faith says such and such about abortion," we communicate to non-Christians that they must accept Christian ideas by a blind exercise of pure will, stepping into the dark. Rather we should insist that such acceptance is a choice to trust what we can have grounds or reason for trusting, and knowledge of what we trust to be true.

But our book is not merely an exposition of the real essence of biblical faith, as important as that is. We go further and explain why there is such an arrangement—a need for faith between us and God—in the first place. We explain in precise and practical detail exactly how to assess the strength of one's confidence in God and his truth, and show how to develop a plan to assure with God's help a life of steady growth in God-confidence. There is great need today for bringing clarity to these issues, and our passion and burden are to do just that in the pages to follow. Christians and non-Christians alike misunderstand what faith is—we don't know how to develop it and lack the tools to assess its strength in our daily lives. By God's mercy, we hope to provide help here that is biblically faithful and practically powerful.

One more thing has been in the center of our attention as we wrote this book: we have attempted to write in such a way that your confident trust in God and his truth will grow *in the very reading of the book*. In the pages to follow, we hope to give you ideas that you can ponder and apply to your life and ministry. But we also want the very act of reading the book to be a means of increasing your confidence. If we have been successful, then you should find your confidence in God growing as you read.

Oh, there's one more thing that may encourage you. We have placed our own confidence in God to be with our readers in such a way that he strengthens their trust beyond what can be explained by simply reading and applying the ideas to follow. And as you will see, we have good grounds for thinking that God is answering our prayers.

Thanksgiving 2007

PART ONE

FACING CHALLENGES
TO OUR FAITH IN GOD

1

WHAT FAITH IS . . .
AND WHAT IT ISN'T

On the evening of December 20, 2005, I (J. P.) was excited with anticipation. To be more accurate, I was fidgety and nervous. In a few minutes, Barbara Walters's much-anticipated prime-time special, *Heaven: Where Is It? How Do We Get There?* was about to be aired. Just a few months earlier, *Dateline NBC* featured a special on demonization and ABC's Elizabeth Vargas hosted an hour-long program on the resurrection of Jesus. As fair as these two programs had been, they shared a common misunderstanding regarding the nature of faith. I was hoping that Barbara Walters's show would be an improvement over the last two programs, but as I watched, my heart sank. Just as with the other two programs, it was fair—but it exhibited the same confused perspective about faith, and no one seemed to notice.

So what was this confused perspective about faith? How did these programs depict the nature of faith? In all three shows, the final conclusion was simply that some people believe in demons, the resurrection of Jesus and heaven, and some don't. But in the final analysis, no one is really right or wrong, and even if someone is right, no one can really know one way or the other. But that doesn't matter because, ultimately, one's choice of a viewpoint is a matter of (blind) faith.

This same type of misunderstanding is evident not only in the media but also in academic and scientific settings, where a hotly contested debate between intelligent design advocates and secularists has been raging over the issue of creation and evolution. Keith Lockitch, a fellow of the Ayn Rand Institute, expressed a common assertion of the secularists in this debate in *The Orange County Register:* "[There is an] essential difference," he wrote, "between reason and faith. In reason, one accepts only conclusions one can prove to be true—conclusions based on sensory evidence and logical inference from such evidence. Faith, on the other hand, is belief unsupported by facts or logic—the blind embrace of ideas despite an absence of evidence or proof."[1]

This misunderstanding about faith has even made its way into our humor. You've heard the old joke about the kid who, when asked what he learned in Sunday school, tells his mom, "We learned that faith is believing what you know isn't so." Or as the notorious sitcom character Archie Bunker put it, "Faith is believing what nobody would believe if it weren't in the Bible."

Unfortunately, this view of faith is no laughing matter. It is a harmful delusion because in one way or another, *everyone*, from the most devout evangelical to the most devout atheist, has faith. Operating without faith of some sort is not an option for anyone—even for the most rational or scientific of persons. This may seem counterintuitive, but, again, the true nature of faith is clouded by so much misunderstanding in our culture that it is difficult to grasp what faith really is and how it is related to knowledge and reason. In the absence of such clarity, there is great confusion about the subject for Christians as well as non-Christians, and this is important because, as we will see in the pages to follow, one of the single most important things about persons is their view of the nature of faith and the precise way they exercise faith.

So then, what exactly is faith? And why in the world is there such an arrangement? One may think, *If I were God, I would set up the world so that things would be clearer than they are and faith would not be so important.* In other words, since faith is part of the deal, there is room for ambiguity and people have an excuse for not believing in God, for not following Jesus. After all, one could argue, you either have faith or you don't. And, in any case, if something is a matter of faith, then at the end of the day, it's a matter of guesswork, of just luck. No one can know what's right, so how can someone be blamed for making an unlucky guess? Besides, faith is such a hard thing to develop, especially for rational people. The whole set-up seems like a bad idea.

These are serious questions, and the issues they raise are at the front edge of life itself. We cannot discuss other important matters without first tackling these. Accordingly, the focus of this chapter will be two central questions: (1) What is faith? (2) Why did God orchestrate it so that faith is so important?

What Is Faith?

Before we begin to understand more fully what the Bible says about faith (chapter four) we need to develop a fuller understanding of the concept of faith itself, as well as address some of the barriers or distractions to growing in our trust in God, the topics of part one, chapters one through three. In this first chapter, we'll discuss three synonyms for faith, three classical theological aspects of faith, three philosophical aspects of faith and how faith eliminates the possibility of moral relativism.

Faith as confidence, trust and reliance. Three key synonyms for *faith* are *confidence, trust* and *reliance.* To have faith in a real estate agent is to have confidence in the agent, to trust and rely on her. To have faith in some alleged truth, say, that cigarettes cause cancer, is to count on this claim, to retain a readiness to act as if the claim is true.

While these insights seem simple at first glance, they are deeply profound and meaningful. The simple observation that faith is confidence or trust is sufficient to dispel the terrible misunderstandings of faith in the broader culture, misunderstandings embedded in the various media confusions cited above. How so? At stake is the relationship between faith on the one hand and reason/evidence/knowledge on the other. In the contemporary understanding, faith and reason are polar opposites such that as one gains evidence or knowledge about something, the room for faith vanishes, and, indeed, there is no need for faith. After all, no one (allegedly) needs to exert faith in the claim that water is H_2O or that gravity keeps us anchored to the ground. But, the argument continues, one needs faith in religious or moral claims because there is no knowledge that these claims are true, no evidence either way for them. But we can see that if faith is essentially *trust* and *confidence,* its proper exercise crucially requires reasons, evidence and knowledge.

In the next chapter, we will examine more fully the relationship between faith and knowledge, but for now, two points should be kept in mind. First, people almost always believe what they think is best supported by the relevant evidence. It is very difficult to believe something one takes to be absurd or with no intellectual support whatever. For example, as the evidence piles up in a trial, all things being equal (e.g., a juror isn't so biased that he or she simply refuses to think about the evidence), a listener's beliefs will be formed according to the evidence. This is the way we were made by God to function. It's also why we are transformed by the renewing of our *minds!* Second, by replacing the term *faith* with *confidence* or one of the other synonyms, it becomes obvious that *faith is trusting what we have reason to believe is true.*

In Scripture, God does not call people to trust in him or some truth he reveals without first revealing himself to those people or providing tests for the truth he reveals (e.g., fulfilled prophecy, a public manifestation of his power, or a manifestation of his presence in New Testament times and subsequently up to the present). In this way, God provides *knowledge* of himself and *attesting credentials for revealed truth.* Confidence (faith) is the appropriate response. Far from being polar opposites, as knowledge of an object (of a real estate agent) or a truth increases (Edie has the highest ranking as a real estate agent in town), so does one's confidence in that object or truth.

While *faith* is a perfectly acceptable biblical term, we recommend that the Christian community use one of the synonyms instead of, or regularly in association with, *faith* because of the horrible, confused way it is currently used and the damaging impact this confused use has on people. Systematic theologian Wayne Grudem has similar thoughts:

> The definition [saving faith is a trust in Jesus Christ as a living person for forgiveness and for eternal life with God] emphasizes *personal trust* in Christ, not just belief in facts about Christ. Because saving faith in Scripture involves this personal trust the word "trust" is a better word to use in contemporary culture than the word "faith" or "belief." . . . The word *trust* is closer to the biblical idea, since we are familiar with trusting persons in everyday life.[2]

For example, compare the different tones conveyed by the names of these three churches: Faith Bible Church, Confidence Bible Church and Trust Bible Church. Throughout most of this book, we have chosen to use the term *God-confidence* in place of the term *faith*.

Three classical theological aspects of faith. Once we recognize that faith is confidence or trust, it is easier to understand why there have been three standard parts of faith regularly taken throughout church history (especially during the Reformation) to flesh out the relevant biblical teaching—faith as knowledge *(notitia)*, faith as assent *(assensus)* and faith as commitment *(fiducia)*.

Notitia: Faith as knowledge. Notitia refers to the content of faith, primarily the assertions of Scripture and theological, doctrinal formulations derived from Scripture. Thus, Jude 3 says, "I felt I had to write and urge you to contend for *the faith* that was once for all entrusted to the saints" (emphasis added). Learning to think theologically, to develop a biblical worldview, to grasp and understand the teachings of Christianity is essential to a vibrant faith. *Notitia* is also defined as knowledge of the meaning of or as understanding the content of doctrinal teaching. This clearly implies that far from being antithetical to faith, knowledge is actually an important ingredient of it. Regarding Jesus' comment about "little faith" in Matthew 17:20, John Nolland explains, "Matthew makes it much more obvious [than other Gospel writers] that it is a journey of growing *understanding* than he does that it is one of growing faith, but the latter is probably thought to be implicit in or at least prepared for by the former."[3] We will examine further this component of faith in the next chapter, but for now we offer the following illustration of the importance of *notitia* for a steady, confident life in God's kingdom.

There is much confusion in our culture today about the nature of forgiveness and its value or lack thereof. Some claim that forgiveness means forgetting the offense, acting like it never happened and denying the natural consequences that followed from it. Further, we sometimes hear people on the evening news opine that forgiveness is an expression of weakness, that it is counterproductive to the healing process, or that one has a right to hang onto anger and vengeance. Now is not the time to discourse about biblical teaching regarding the nature of forgiveness—what it is and what it is not—and the spiritual, social and psychological advantages that follow from a heart of forgiveness.[4] For now, we rest content to make one point: If we take *notitia* to involve the idea that the Bible provided knowledge of the various topics about which it speaks, then the disciples of Jesus possess something precious indeed: genuine, rock-solid knowledge about the nature and benefits of forgiveness.

Assensus: Faith as agreement. Assensus refers to personal assent to, awareness of or agreement with the truth of Christian teaching, and, again, it is primarily intellectual, though as we shall see in chapter three, there are clear affective and psychological components to *assensus*. Medieval theologians distinguished varying degrees of assent to something, with "full assent without hesitation" as the strongest form. The important thing is that it is not enough to *grasp* the contents of Christian teaching; one must also *accept* the fact that this teaching is true.

However, there is great confusion among God's people about what it means to accept a teaching as true and how one goes about doing this. A major burden of this book is to help correct this situation. Before leaving the topic, however, and as an introduction to our conversation about these matters later, we mention three absolutely central things to keep in mind when you ponder what it is to actually believe some biblical teaching. First, one must distinguish among (1) *unbelief* (a willful and sinful setting of oneself against a biblical teaching), (2) *doubt* (an intellectual, emotional or psychological hindrance to a more secure confidence in some teaching or in God himself—I believe something but just have doubts) and (3) *lack of belief* (I don't believe something but know I should and want to—I need help).

Second, as we shall see, not all doubt is explicitly intellectual. There are deep affective, psychological issues involved as well. For example, if you had attachment issues as a child and were not regularly connected to warm, strong, loving parents, you may have difficulty believing that God the Father is tender and kind. If so, then what is essential for developing greater confidence in God includes participating in healthy relationships and engaging in spiritual formation exercises, perhaps also being involved in therapy.[5]

Third, confidence is not an all-or-nothing affair. If one does not have confidence in something, he or she may lack trust to varying degrees. The same may be said for having trust in something.

Thus, we now have a stifling, stagnating situation in the evangelical community: People do not feel safe in expressing doubt or lack of belief about some doctrinal point—even the question of whether they actually believe in God. The result is that people hide what they actually believe from others, and even from themselves, all the while continuing to use faith-talk to avoid being socially ostracized in their local fellowship. Because we do not fully understand *assensus* (and *fiducia;* see below), we have unintentionally created a situation in which people do not know how to distinguish what they believe from what they *say* they believe. Thus, they substitute community jargon for authentic trust.

To effectively address this situation, we must create safe, honest, nondefensive fellowships in which people are given permission to be on a faith journey, with all the warts, messiness and setbacks that are part of such a journey. We must also address general and specific intellectual doubts, provide insights about the affective, emotional hindrances to growth in confidence in God, and become more intentional about bearing credible witnesses to each other regarding answers to prayer and other supernatural experiences that strengthen faith.

Fiducia: Faith as commitment. Finally, *fiducia* involves personal commitment to its object, whether to a truth or a person. *Fiducia* is essentially a matter of the will, but because Christianity is a relationship with a Person and not just commitment to a set of truths (though this is, of course, essential), the capacity to develop emotional intimacy and to discern the inner movements of feeling, intuition and God's Spirit in the soul is crucial to maintaining and cultivating commitment to God.

Merely exhorting people to be more committed to God—"just have more faith"—seldom produces greater confidence and dedicated trust in God. Rather, *what is needed is a realistic picture of a flourishing life lived deeply in tune with God's kingdom*—a life that is so utterly compelling that failure to exercise greater commitment to life in that kingdom will feel like a foolish, tragic missed opportunity for entering into something truly dramatic and desirable.

These three classical distinctions—*noticia, assensus* and *fiducia*—are indispensable to helping us build a broader understanding of the concept of faith. For a chart that summarizes our discussion, see table 1.1.

Table 1.1. Three Classical Theological Aspects of Faith

Classical Aspect	Description
Noticia	Content of faith, such as Scriptures or theological doctrines; understanding the meaning of this content
Assensus	Personal awareness of, assent to or agreement with the truth of certain propositions
Fiducia	Willful commitment to living a life that reflects this truth

Three philosophical aspects of faith. Besides these classic components of faith, a robust understanding of faith requires insight into three philosophical aspects.

Degrees of faith. As we mentioned above, the presence or absence of belief, trust and confidence comes in *degrees*. Consider any candidate for belief, for example, that the Cubs and White Sox will never compete in a World Series. There are three ways of relating to this claim. You can disbelieve it, you can believe it, or you can be counterbalanced, literally 50/50 with no leaning either way. So if you believe something, you are 51-100 percent sure it's true; if you disbelieve it, you are 51-100 percent sure it's false. The same goes with having confidence in an object or a person. For example, if you trust a person, your confidence in them ranges from 51 percent to 100 percent.

The importance of these insights cannot be overestimated. Great harm is done to people if we simplistically harangue them by saying, "Hey, you either believe this stuff or you don't! It's that simple. So take it or leave it!" Of course, since we are seldom literally 50/50 about most of our ideas, especially Christian ones, there is some truth to these assertions. Apart from being counterbalanced about a claim, we usually do either believe or disbelieve some proposition. But these assertions are simplistic and exhibit a gross representation of the subtlety of faith.

Usually, these assertions are taken to mean that you are 100 percent convinced about a proposition; you are totally committed; you have no hesitation or wavering at all regarding, say, the power of prayer; or you really don't believe it. Much guilt and discouragement is produced from such attitudes. The truth is that you can actually believe something but stand in need of increasing your confidence in it. Similarly, in evangelistic encounters, if one helps move a non-Christian from being in a state of 80 percent to 40 percent disbelief, then even though the person did not become a believer, great good was accomplished. It follows from the fact that *confidence comes in degrees,* that in order to grow in Christ, it is not enough to assess what we do and do not believe. Rather, it is crucial to assess our degree of belief. For example, how strong is your confidence about these claims: (1) It is possible to actually forgive your enemies. (2) God accepts and wants to use you in spite of repeated, habitual sin on your part. And so on. If we are going to be intentional about cultivating our reliance on God, we will have to assess the strength of our actual beliefs, develop ways to remove hindrances to their development and find tools for their cultivation.

Confidence in and confidence that. Another aspect to faith is the difference between "confidence in" and "confidence that." The former, "confidence in," is directed toward some object—either an impersonal one, such as confidence in a car, a medicine or a particular mutual fund, or toward a person, such as your doctor, God or your spouse. The latter, "confidence that," is directed toward an alleged truth, a proposition, an idea—believing that Jesus is the Son of God, that stealing is wrong or that the Missouri River is muddy.

Two important things follow from the distinction between "confidence in" and "confidence that." For one thing, the proper value of each rests on the worthiness of its object. Regarding "confidence in," its proper value is derived from the reality of its object and the object's dependability or trustworthiness. In most cases, the effectiveness, reliability or virtue/skill of the object is at issue. Regarding "confidence that," its proper value derives from the fact that the object—a particular claim—is actually true and not false. Some people claim that the value of faith lies in the personal benefits that come from the act of believing itself, not in the reality and nature of the object or the truth of the belief. If this were the case, beliefs would only be like placebos—medication having no active ingredient (e.g., a sugar pill) used in medical experiments.

But this claim about belief itself is false because if a person found out that some object either did not really exist or did exist but wasn't at all reliable, or that some belief turns out to be false, then the person should immediately reject the belief. In fact, that is what people will actually do regardless of what they say because people cannot believe something they really think is false. To continue to say you believe something that is not real or is false is to live in a fantasy world. People who cannot distinguish fantasy from reality or who don't care about the difference are not proper guides for teaching us what faith should look like. The nature of the object of faith, whether trustworthy or true, is essential to any valid belief. Faith is only as good as the nature of its object. A chair with a broken leg won't hold you up no matter how much faith you have to sit in it. The integrity of faith's object is the key.

The second implication of the distinction between "confidence in" and "confidence that" is that while truth is an important aspect of biblical faith, faith goes beyond accepting certain truths and crucially involves "confidence in" and reliance upon a Person—the Triune God. This is the "confidence in" dimension. Among other things, this means that the growth or stagnation of such confidence is intimately wrapped up in the dynamics of interpersonal relationships, including factors conducive to experiencing intimacy with others, especially God. Learning to trust a person, and even God, involves learning to face one's emotions, learning to feel things instead of being split off from them, learning to deal with defense mechanisms such as projection or repression, and having time to be quiet and unhurried. True faith involves both aspects—confidence in and confidence that something is the case. These issues are so critical that we address them further in chapter three.

How beliefs change. The final aspect of faith has to do with how beliefs change. In essence, persons do not have *direct control* over what they do and do not believe (or regarding the strength of their beliefs), but they do have *indirect control* over their beliefs. Put differently, *one's beliefs (and their strength) are not directly subject to one's free will, though other activities that indirectly produce (or strengthen) belief are subject to one's free will.* If someone were to offer you $5,000 to believe that a pink elephant is standing next to you at this moment, you *could not* believe such a thing even if you tried. Similarly, you could not choose on the spot to believe that Bill Clinton was never president of the United States, that germs aren't real or that torturing little babies for the fun of it is morally permissible. This is why it doesn't help much to exhort people to believe things. In fact, it is a frustrating waste of time to try to believe something (or increase your belief) *directly.* Failure is virtually guaranteed. That's the bad news.

The good news is that you can indirectly control what you believe and how strongly you believe it by freely choosing to do certain things that develop God-confidence as a byproduct. Throughout this book, we will look at things within your control that you can do to deepen your God-confidence.

The three classical aspects of faith (*noticia, assensus* and *fiducia*), along with these three philosophical aspects of faith, move us toward a fuller understanding of what the concept of faith entails. Table 1.2 visually encapsulates the three philosophical aspects of faith.

Table 1.2. Three Philosophical Aspects of Faith

Philosophical aspect	Description
Degrees of belief	Beliefs come in degrees 1-100 percent, not as either-or, presence or absence.
Confidence in and confidence that	*Confidence in* is directed toward an object or person. *Confidence that* is directed toward an alleged truth.
Changing beliefs	Beliefs are changed indirectly rather than directly.

Faith and moral relativism. We have seen that an essential part of faith and belief is the idea that the thing believed is true. If I say "I believe that 2 + 2 = 4" or "I believe abortion is wrong" or "I believe that the sore on your face is skin cancer," then what I am saying is, "I take such and such to be true to some degree between 51 percent and 100 percent." When we say that some assertion is true ("grass is green"), we are saying that this assertion corresponds to or matches with reality (that grass is actually green). Reality is what makes an assertion true or false, and truth obtains when an assertion actually corresponds to the way reality is.

Now, having a true idea is not a function of whether you can tell or prove it's true. If everyone were blind, and grass was actually green, then "grass is green" would be true even if no one believed it or even if everyone believed it but couldn't tell one way or another if they were correct. Evidence is related to whether we *know* that some idea ("grass is green") is true. But reality itself is what *makes* something true. Thus, if one believes that grass is green, then one takes it to be true to some degree that reality objectively corresponds to this claim, that it is an objective fact that grass really is green. So, when someone says that they believe something or that such and such is their opinion, they are saying that they take the claim to be objectively true to some degree that may fall far short of certainty but which, nevertheless, would be higher than 50 percent.

There is a crucial implication in these insights: When people claim that they believe something is true for them, that in their opinion such and such is the case, they may very well be expressing a commitment to an absolute truth, and not be true relativists, that is, someone who believes something may be true for one person but false for another who does not believe it. For example, if I say, "In my opinion, that sore on your face is skin cancer" or "I believe for me that the sore is skin cancer," I am saying that it is an objective truth that the sore is skin cancer. Now if this is true, then how should we understand phrases like "in my opinion" or "I believe such and such *for me*"?

These phrases express the idea that the speaker is unsure of his view, that he cannot defend it, and that even if he is wrong he doesn't want to have to defend his views and doesn't want you questioning him. Most of the time when people say things like "Prochoice is correct for me" or "In my opinion, in my beliefs, I am prochoice" they are not really expressing relativism even if they think they are! Why? Because the very act of saying that this is one's belief or opinion implies that they take the belief to be true. The person is saying, "I think the prochoice position is objectively true for everyone, but I can't defend this, I am not an expert, so let me say this without having to back it up." This is like saying, "That is skin cancer to me" or "In my opinion, that's skin cancer." The individual is not really being a relativist. She is *not* saying that the sore actually becomes skin cancer for her simply because she believes it to be so but it may not actually be skin cancer to someone else if they don't believe it.

That is usually the case when someone utters the phrase "in my opinion." But the genuine relativist thinks that believing something actually does make it true for the believer. Furthermore, the true relativist assertion (for example, "abortion is wrong") is then both true (for the believer) and false (for someone who doesn't believe it) at the same time relative to the two people—no one is really wrong. This is a radical idea, and it's pretty crazy in most cases. But genuine relativism is much rarer than most assume because the nature of faith is such that a claim to believe something implies a commitment to its objective truth. When people add phrases like "in my opinion," "such and such is true to me," they are usually not expressing real relativism. Rather, they are claiming that the assertion is objectively true but that they don't really know enough to be able to defend their views adequately to someone who questions it. They are expressing low confidence, 51 percent, in what they nevertheless believe to be true.

In sum, when a person has faith in or believes something, he or she takes the thing believed to be true. But a person can have faith in or believe something without being completely certain that he or she is right. Sometimes people say, "I believe such and such for me" and thereby express a form of relativism, but more often the person is actually expressing a lack of certainty about what he or she actually believes to be true.

Why Faith?

We have examined the nature of faith from several angles. But at this point, one has to wonder: Why did God set up things so that there would have to be such a thing as faith in the first place? Why is it so essential for relating to him, and why does so much hang on it, including where one will spend eternity? Why didn't God make it more evident that he's really there, so faith wouldn't be so important and no one would have any excuses? After all, some people claim that if God were more evident, they would believe in him, but faith is too risky. And some people have faith and some people don't—so it seems arbitrary. Wasn't there a better way to arrange all this besides hanging the entire set-up on such a thin thread as faith?

We encounter these questions and complaints regularly, and they trouble many people. But we think that the questions can be adequately answered, and, in fact, they represent some real confusion about faith itself. Three things clue us in to the necessity of faith.

The hiddenness of God. First, it is important to come to terms with the biblical teaching about the hiddenness of God.[6] God is not interested in merely getting people to believe he is there. That's why he doesn't write something in the sky for all to see. Rather, he is interested in forming a community of people—his kingdom covenant people—who have entered that community voluntarily and uncoerced, and they have done so for the right reasons, among which include the desire to be with and like God himself. To accomplish this, God regularly makes his manifest presence—a presence that is detectable by those for whom the manifestation was given—hidden so people can be free to choose for or against God and this community.

To clarify, the existence of God is not itself hidden. The universe is not religiously ambiguous. It is clear that a personal, holy God exists, and, in fact, there is *knowledge* for anyone who wants it that this God is real. Christians differ over exactly how it is a person can have knowledge that God is real. Some appeal to the evidence of creation. Those who appeal to creation are divided about whether knowledge of God is self-evident and intuitively obvious from creation or knowledge of God requires theistic arguments based on creation. Others believe we are born with innate knowledge that God exists. Still others think that knowledge of God results from the fact that our idea of and belief in God are formed by our rational and sensory faculties when they are functioning properly. However, regardless of divisions about *how* we know that God is real, the Bible clearly teaches that there is knowledge of the existence of God (Psalm 19; Romans 1).

What is hidden is God's manifest presence and some of his intentions. John Wimber used to spell *faith* "R-I-S-K." And he was correct. However, contrary to what some liberal, secularized theologians claim, the risk of faith is not about whether God exists or Christianity is true. These are items of knowledge. Rather, the risk is about stepping out day by day in service of the kingdom and in reliance on its King, often while being in the dark about where God is and how he is (or isn't!) moving in one's circumstances. This sort of faith-risk is made possible by the hiddenness of God.

Faith as the foundation of life. The second response is that, in light of the fuller understanding of the nature of faith provided above, it becomes evident that faith—confidence in and confidence that—is the very rail upon which we live our lives. We almost always act up (or down) to what we really believe and to the strength of those beliefs. What we do and do not trust, what we actually think is true and false, what we do and do not have a readiness to rely upon—these constitute the very essence of the sort of person we are. These things make up the roadmap in our mind, our emotions and our bodily habits that inform our character; constitute our habits of thought and feeling; and shape the priorities and behaviors that make up the very substance of our lives. Thus, given a correct and full grasp of the nature of faith itself, it becomes evident that a person's faith may well be the single most important thing about him or her.

The questions listed above usually give expression to the tragic cultural misunderstanding of faith illustrated by the various media events chronicled at the beginning of the chapter. If faith were, indeed, a blind, arbitrary leap in the dark that has no basis in reason, evidence or knowledge, then we would agree that these questions have no adequate answer and God would have chosen a pretty bad set-up for running his world. But God doesn't make mistakes, and this is a grotesque distortion of faith, a sad fact made more grotesque by how widely accepted the view is. Once we gain a more accurate view of faith—one in which faith is rooted in knowledge—it becomes evident that God's plan for the world is a not a mistake.

Faith and persons. But all of this, while helpful in showing the value of faith, given that there is such an arrangement, does not explain why the arrangement is there in the first place. Why is there such a thing as faith? The answer is grounded in the nature of persons: we flourish in the presence of trust from others, offering confidence and trust is one way to show respect to and value other persons, and reliance on and confidence in another are essential to the way persons work together and cooperate with each other. Try to imagine what personal relationships would be like if there were no such things as trust and expressions of confidence in others. For example, in the arena of business, trust is what makes any business transaction possible, what economists and political scientists call "social capital." As Francis Fukuyama writes,

> Social capital can be defined simply as an instantiated set of informal values or norms shared among members of a group that permits them to cooperate with one another. If members of the group come to expect that others will behave reliably and honestly, then they will come to *trust* one another. Trust acts like a lubricant that makes any group or organization run more efficiently.[7]

Imagine what would happen to personal flourishing, individually and communally, if there were no such thing as trust. When we recall that faith is not blind choice but is trust, reliance and confidence, it becomes clear that the existence of faith is merely one important aspect of the nature of persons and the proper way they relate to one another. Furthermore, God-confidence is fundamental to living well in this universe, as Hebrews 11:6 teaches: "And without faith it is impossible to please God, because anyone who comes to him must believe that he exists and that he rewards those who earnestly seek him."

Now that we have a good introduction to the concept of faith, in the final two chapters of part one, we'll explore more about intellectual doubts (chapter two) and emotional barriers to faith (chapter three). Then in part two, we'll focus on increasing our expectations of God, building a case for how our God-confidence can grow. In chapter four, we'll look at Jesus' teaching about faith and some amazing New Testament promises believers need to examine. In chapter five, we provide some contemporary examples and case studies that can help us increase our God-confidence to rely on what Jesus teaches about faith. Finally, we tackle one practical arena in which we can grow in our confidence in God, making life decisions as we seek God's guidance (chapter six). We hope this final chapter will help expand your perspective on the various ways God personally communicates to believers, through his Word as well as other means, in order to provide divine guidance in which we can place our trust.

> *To trust Him is not a leap in the dark, but it is a*
> *venture none the less. It is a venture of courage and not of despair,*
> *of insight and not of bewilderment.*
>
> P. T. FORSYTH, *THE CREATIVE THEOLOGY OF P. T. FORSYTH*

Questions for Personal Reflection or Group Discussion

1. At the beginning of this chapter, the authors described several instances in which the media presented a confused perspective about faith. Can you think of similar examples that you have per-

sonally seen or heard in films, contemporary music or television? If so, what was your response?

2. The authors discussed six aspects of faith—three classical aspects (*noticia, assensus, fiducia,* table 1.1) and three philosophical aspects (degrees of faith, confidence in and confidence that, and how beliefs are changed, table 1.2). Try to describe these aspects in your own words. How do these aspects change or influence the way you understand the concept of faith? What do you see as the implications for living out these concepts?

3. Because of the ambiguous nature of the term *faith* in contemporary language, the authors suggested that the term *faith* be replaced with other terms, such as *God-confidence*. Do you think using synonyms such as these can bring clarity to what we mean when we refer to the concept of biblical faith?

4. Have you ever wondered why faith is a necessary part of the makeup of the world? Do you agree or disagree with the claim that faith is the foundation upon which we live our lives? Why or why not?

2

DEALING WITH DOUBTS

Distractions of the Head

A pervasive misperception in contemporary American culture is that people of religious faith, particularly Christians, are intellectually inferior to those who do not have religious faith. Television personality Bill Maher, host of *Real Time with Bill Maher*, recently claimed that Christians, along with all religious people, suffer from a neurological disorder that "stops people from thinking." When pressed about his claim, he further commented, "When people say to me, 'You hate America,' I don't hate America. I love America. I am just embarrassed that it has been taken over by evangelicals, by people who do not believe in science and rationality."[1]

And Bill Maher is not the only one leveling such charges against Christians. For the most part, the media, the entertainment industry (including television, movies and music) and even some of those in the top leadership positions in the country frequently perpetuate the image of the Christian as naive or ignorant. With such opposition on all these fronts, it's easy to see why many people are embarrassed to be Christian believers. We are regularly sold the idea that unbelief is tough-minded and belief is fuzzy-minded, that unbelief is rational and belief is gullible. We may even be tempted to assume that among the intellectual heavyweights of the world there are no Christians, that all are opposed to any form of belief. As Dallas Willard noted,

> The crushing weight of the secular outlook . . . permeates or pressures every thought we have today. Sometimes it even forces those who self-identify as Christian teachers to set aside Jesus' plain statements about the reality and total relevance of the kingdom of God and replace them with philosophical speculations whose only recommendation is their consistency with a "modern" [i.e., contemporary] mind-set. The powerful though vague and unsubstantiated presumption is that *something has been found out* that renders a spiritual understanding of reality in the manner of Jesus simply foolish to those who are "in the know."[2]

Embarrassment is one of the worst feelings we can have. Think back to an embarrassing moment in your life. Can you remember how red your face felt? Doing a Houdini disappearing act seemed the only way out. Have you ever been embarrassed for being a Christian? Honestly, intellectual embarrassment—looking stupid, appearing ignorant—may be the worst kind of embarrassment. That's one reason why people fear public speaking even more than they fear the dentist—they're afraid of sharing something with a group they perceive to contain people much more knowledgeable than themselves. We want to avoid looking ignorant. And if being a Christian is identified with being ignorant or backward, we will be afraid of witnessing and it will be harder for us to stand up for our Christian beliefs without coming across as defensive.

Such fear is the very opposite of trust. And this fear is why so many Christians retreat to a "blind faith." After all, if Christianity involves knowledge and a person doesn't know what he believes and cannot defend it well, that person risks being inadequate and risks being called ignorant. But if faith is just a private arbitrary choice, a step in the dark, who can criticize that? A person can say anything he or she wants, and if challenged, he or she can retreat into safety by simply pointing out that all people have their private beliefs and these beliefs are their own, personal beliefs. As we saw in the last chapter, this is, unfortunately, what the popular view of faith is all about.

But the price we pay for such comfort is pretty high. For one thing, the difference between Christianity and atheism or Buddhism is reduced to the superficial difference of personal preferences, like between those who prefer Windows PC and those who prefer Mac. It's just a matter of taste. For another thing, a retreat to private feelings keeps a person from honestly facing doubts and working through them, with the result that after years of this approach, she can no longer distinguish what she really believes from what she says she believes in front of others. In this case, one will be plagued with ongoing doubts and lack genuine confidence in God or commitment to some specific issue in the Christian life. When this happens, people can often suppress their doubts. We are masters at self-deception. But we must never forget that James hit it on the head when he observed that those who persist in unresolved doubt will lack genuine faith (James 1:5-8). The result of this, he correctly noted, is a life of instability, a life that cannot make decisions and stick to them, a life that cannot be at peace or be confident in convictions. And that's a high price to pay.

As we saw in chapter one, this popular view of faith is not consonant with common sense or with a Christian understanding of God-confidence, nor is it consonant with the reliance in God that Jesus himself exhibited and taught, as we'll see in chapter four. God-confidence is not opposed to knowledge of reality, reason and evidence. On the contrary, it is grounded in this knowledge. The good news is that God-confidence does not require you to be ignorant, to hide from or avoid facing tough questions, to set aside intellectual honesty and just believe blindly and with little or no understanding of what you believe or why you believe it. Historically and presently, Christianity has been and often remains the champion of reason and knowledge.

However, it's sometimes hard to know how to address intellectual doubts. How, exactly, does one grow in God-confidence by dealing responsibly with intellectual doubts? In this chapter, we will analyze these "distractions of the head" and suggest ways to deal with these doubts and to grow in God-confidence.

The Essential Role of Knowledge

Surprisingly, the Bible has as much to say about knowledge of God and his Word as it does about trust. And even though we may know them in different ways, according to Christianity, we know (or at least can know) that God exists and is who the Bible says he is. And we know (or at least can know) that Jesus is the Son of God and the Bible is his Word, every bit as much as we know (or at least can know) the chemical structure of water or the fact that George Washington was a U.S. president. No blind faith here! Consider this small sampling of biblical teaching on knowledge.[3]

> But Abram said, "O Sovereign LORD, how can I *know* that I will gain possession of it?" So the LORD said to him . . . (Genesis 15:8-9)

> Then Moses said, "This is how you will *know* that the LORD has sent me to do all these things and that it was not my idea." (Numbers 16:28)

> *Acknowledge* [lit., know] and take to heart this day that the LORD is God in heaven above and on the earth below. There is no other. (Deuteronomy 4:39)

> The lips of the righteous *know* what is fitting. (Proverbs 10:32)

Know and *understand* this. (Daniel 9:25)

The *knowledge* of the secrets of the kingdom of heaven has been given to you, but not to them. (Matthew 13:11)

You are in error because you do not *know* the Scriptures or the power of God. (Matthew 22:29)

Anyone who chooses to do the will of God *will find out* [lit., will know] whether my teaching comes from God or whether I speak on my own. (John 7:17 TNIV)

Believe the miracles, that you may *know* and *understand* that the Father is in me, and I in the Father. (John 10:38)

This is the disciple who testifies to these things and who wrote them down. We *know* that his testimony is true. (John 21:24)

And we *know* that in all things God works for the good of those who love him, who have been called according to his purpose. (Romans 8:28)

We *know* that an idol is nothing at all in the world and that there is no God but one. (1 Corinthians 8:4)

Now we *know* that if the earthly tent we live in is destroyed, we have a building from God, an eternal house in heaven, not built by human hands. (2 Corinthians 5:1)

We *know* that the law is good if one uses it properly. (1 Timothy 1:8)

We *know* that we have come to *know* him if we obey his commands. (1 John 2:3—a matchless example of propositional knowledge, personal knowledge and moral ground)

Even now many antichrists have come. This is how we *know* it is the last hour. (1 John 2:18)

But we *know* that when [Christ] appears, we shall be like him. (1 John 3:2)

This is how we *know* that we love the children of God: by loving God and carrying out his commands. (1 John 5:2)

I write these things to you who believe in the name of the Son of God so that you may *know* that you have eternal life. (1 John 5:13)

And if we *know* that he hears us—whatever we ask—we *know* that we have what we asked of him. (1 John 5:15)

Yet these people speak abusively against whatever they *do not understand* [lit., know]; and what things they *do understand* [lit., know] by instinct, like unreasoning animals—these are the very things that destroy them. (Jude 10 TNIV)

These Scriptures remind us that we can know an amazing range of things, including that God exists, that there is such a thing as life after death, that biblical teachings are true, and that certain things are right and others are wrong. We are not left in a position of hoping or "merely believing" that these things are so. Furthermore, we can also have personal, intimate, experiential *knowledge* of God. Knowledge plays an essential role in the Christian life. Common sense tells us that if we are going to be good at anything—math, tennis, parenting—we have to *know* something and derive our confidence from such knowledge. The same is true about getting good at life, being close to God and living in a way that makes him happy! In his comment on 2 Corinthians 5:7, "We live by faith, not by sight," Scott Hafemann notes that

"faith" is trusting in the promises of God for the future, not in spite of what one knows but *because* of what one knows. The lack of "sight" in this passage does not refer to the uncertain *basis* of faith but to the fact that the consummation of God's promises has not yet been realized. Paul's point in [2 Corinthians] 5:7 is not epistemological (i.e., that we can only know things "by faith," since we have no certain reasons for believing, i.e., no "sight"), but eschatological (i.e., that we live in the present by trusting God's promises for the future, the down payment of which we are already experiencing in the Spirit).[4]

But what is knowledge? *Knowledge is either an accurate experiential awareness of reality or a true belief about reality based on adequate grounds.* If I accurately see a lamp before me, then I have knowledge of the lamp by being acquainted with or aware of it. This same sort of experiential knowledge of God and of his guidance is available to us through the testimony of God's Spirit and our accurate awareness of God in moments of worship and meditation.[5] Moreover, if I know that George Washington was a U.S. president, then I have a true belief that George Washington was a U.S. president and this belief is based on adequate, though not necessarily conclusive, grounds. In this case, my belief that George Washington was a U.S. president is based on testimonial and historical grounds.

Similarly, when we have knowledge of various doctrinal truths grounded in the Bible; the physical creation; the evidence of fulfilled prophecy in Scripture; the scientific, philosophical and historical evidence that forms part of apologetics; or the Spirit's testimony, we have true beliefs about these things based on a wide variety of adequate grounds for those beliefs. The degree of adequacy of those grounds can vary, as not all of these are equal in the grounds they provide. Nor is the type of grounds the same in all cases (e.g., sometimes religious experience, sometimes historical evidence or philosophical argumentation). But if we remember certain aspects of knowledge, it will be obvious that beliefs grounded in more limited degrees of adequacy (such as religious experience or testimony of the Holy Spirit) may still count as knowledge.

Two Critical Aspects of Knowledge

There are two critical aspects of knowledge that we must keep in mind in order to grow in God-confidence. First, to know something one does not have to be absolutely certain or assured about the issue in question. If I know that George Washington was president of the United States, it is consistent with such knowledge that I admit I could be wrong, that I could, at one time or another, doubt the truth of the assertion. Like God-confidence, knowledge comes in degrees. One can know something (be accurately aware of it or have a true belief based on good grounds) to increasingly greater degrees. That's why it makes sense to say, "I knew such and such was true, but now I am even more convinced about it." In fact, take a look at the following passages:

> Then you may *be sure* [lit., know for certain] that the LORD your God will no longer drive out these nations before you. (Joshua 23:13)

> *Be assured* [lit., know for certain], however, that if you put me to death, you will bring the guilt of innocent blood on yourselves and on this city and on those who live in it, for in truth the LORD has sent me to you to speak all these words in your hearing. (Jeremiah 26:15)

> Those who *think they know* something *do not yet know* as they *ought to know.* (1 Corinthians 8:2 TNIV)

> For of this you can *be sure:* No immoral, impure or greedy person—such a person is an idolater—has any inheritance in the kingdom of Christ and of God. (Ephesians 5:5 TNIV)

All these texts assume a distinction between knowing and knowing *for sure.* If such a distinction were not real, then it would be redundant to use the phrase "know for certain" since knowledge would itself include certainty. And the distinction between knowing and knowing for certain implies that there is such a thing as genuine knowledge that is not completely, 100-percent certain.

Why is this so important? Because it raises the bar way too high to require that one can only claim to know important things relevant to Christianity when one is *completely certain*. Moreover, the mere presence of doubt does not mean that one does not know the thing in question. Finally, having a meaningful criterion allows us to set before ourselves the lifetime goal of knowing God and his Word with increasingly greater degrees of certainty without having to label our earlier stages as ones in which we did not possess the relevant knowledge.

The quest to know God experientially and to know what and why one believes certain truths is not at odds with the cultivation of a growing God-confidence but is, rather, essential to it. To be sure, knowledge can make a person prideful. But as was modeled in Paul's own life, the solution to this problem is not ignorance but humility. In all honesty, the more we grow to know God and ourselves, the less we have to be prideful about!

So then, while certainty can be wonderful and appropriate, in some cases certainty is not required to have knowledge. And when there are genuine conflicts among godly interpreters of the Bible about the meaning of certain passages, then even if one claims, perhaps accurately, to know the correct view of the passage, it would be a stretch to say one had such knowledge *with certainty!*

Second, you can know something without *knowing that* you know it. To grasp why this observation is so crucial, we need to reflect on the fact that confidence grows in a person not only because he has knowledge about something, but even more importantly, because the person *knows* that he has such knowledge. Most people know many things relevant to a Christian worldview, like the fact that there is a God, life after death, or absolute morality. Sadly, because our culture is dominated by naturalistic and postmodern assumptions that these things cannot be items of real knowledge, many people would not acknowledge that they know these matters even though they do know them to some degree.

We grow in God-confidence by knowing that we know things and not *merely* by knowing them. This is pretty obvious if we reflect on daily life. Consider Nicole, who is going to a job interview. She may actually know the answers to a set of questions given to her before the interview, but if she does not think she prepared hard enough for the interview, she may not *know* she knows those answers. Or, it might be that she can't admit to herself that she knows the answers. That may happen, too. But in the example we are considering, Nicole doesn't really know that she possesses knowledge of the answers to the interview questions even though she does possess it. Now, in this case, how do you think she will approach the interview? It's pretty clear that she will lack a good bit of confidence. Why? Her lack of confidence isn't due to her lack of knowledge of the answers. She has that. No, it is due to her lack of knowledge that she actually knows those answers, and it is this lack of what philosophers call second-order knowledge—knowing that one knows something— that robs her of confidence.

This is why it is so important that we have faithful Christian scholars in our community and that people know they are there. We can't all be experts at everything, so knowledge of their presence strengthens our God-confidence by giving us assurance that we actually know the things we claim to know.

Christianity is a knowledge tradition, not a "mere belief" tradition, and in order to grow our God-confidence, one of the important tasks before us is to grow in our knowledge of God and his Word. Ultimately, for this to be possible, we must learn to handle our intellectual doubts.

Plausibility Structures and God-Confidence

Look at figure 2.1 and notice what you see. Notice that the right vertical line looks longer than the one on the left even though their lengths are the same. Why? Because we see these shapes hundreds of times a day (the right diagram is the inside corner of a room; the left is the outside corner of a building), we are unconsciously used to seeing them as three-dimensional objects, and so we unconsciously try to adjust to the two-dimensionality of the figures on the page to our more general experience. In this case, our habits of perception and thought shape what we see. When this diagram is shown to people in cultures having no square or rectangular buildings, they have no such subconscious habits and they see the horizontal lines accurately as being of equal length.

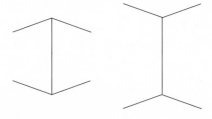

Figure 2.1. Optical illusion

There's an important lesson in this. Every culture has a set of background assumptions—we can call it a plausibility structure—that sets a tone or a framework for what people think, how they feel and how they act. It directs what they will entertain as plausible, what they will habitually notice or disregard without thinking about what they are doing, and how they form and retain their beliefs. This plausibility structure is so widespread and subtle that people usually don't even know it is there even though it hugely impacts their perspective on the world. The plausibility structure is composed of thoughts (e.g., scientists are smart; religious people are gullible and dumb), symbols (a flag being burned, a picture of Paris Hilton, tattoos), music and so forth. It is so deeply internalized and widely adopted that is it taken for granted. It is so subconscious that it is seldom noticed.

For example, a book published with Oxford University Press may be taken by a reader to be more credible and to exhibit greater scholarship than a book by an evangelical publisher, even though this assumption is clearly false in certain cases. Again, if you walk on campus at, say, the University of Southern California and Biola University, the age differences, the buildings, the relative size of the libraries, and the fact that USC professors appear more frequently on news programs than do Biola professors may influence you to believe that USC classes are more intellectually substantial and a USC education is more intellectually rigorous than one at Biola.

Here's the problem this raises for trust in God. Without even knowing it, we all carry with us this cultural map, this background set of assumptions, and our self-talk—the things that form our default beliefs (ones we naturally accept without argument), the things we are embarrassed to believe (if they run contrary to the authorities in our cultural map), and related matters—create a natural set of doubts about Christianity. Most of these factors are things people are not even aware of. In fact, if this cultural map is brought to people's attention, they would most likely disown it even though, in fact, it constitutes the internalized ideas that actually shape what people do and don't believe.

Our current Western cultural plausibility structure elevates science and scorns and mocks religion, especially Christian teaching. As a result, believers in Western cultures do not as readily believe the supernatural worldview of the Bible in comparison with their Third World brothers and sisters. As Christian cultural anthropologist Charles Kraft observes:

In comparison to other societies, Americans and other North Atlantic peoples are *naturalistic*. Non-Western peoples are frequently concerned about the activities of supernatural beings. Though many Westerners retain a vague belief in God, most deny that other supernatural beings even exist. The wide-ranging supernaturalism of most of the societies of the world is absent for most of our people. . . . Our focus is on the natural world, with little or no attention paid to the supernatural world.[6]

So what can we do about this problem? Below we will examine how to handle certain specific intellectual doubts. These kinds of doubts are very clear. People are even self-conscious about them and can write them down on paper. These can be resolved by finding a satisfying answer to them.

In contrast, other doubts are unknowingly fed by ideas absorbed from the plausibility structure of the surrounding culture. People with these kinds of doubts are unaware of how they have been influenced by the assumptions made by the surrounding culture (and, as we said above, they may not even recognize those assumptions even when made explicit). Even though such assumptions are usually easy to answer, finding such answers does not, by itself, resolve the doubts. This can only be done by making these cultural assumptions explicit, by exposing them for the intellectual frauds they actually are, and by being vigilant in keeping them before one's mind and spotting their presence in the ordinary reception of input each day from newspapers, magazines, office conversation, television, movies and so on. Said differently, it is not enough to find good answers to these doubts as it is for more specific intellectual problems. *The real solution here is the conscious formation of alternative, countercultural ways of seeing, thinking and being present* in the world. If this is not done, these background assumptions will bully us Christians to live secular lives, and they will squeeze the spiritual life out of us.

Here are seven of the main doubt-inducing background assumptions of our culture:

1. It is smarter to doubt things than to believe them. Smart people are skeptical. People who find faith easy are simplistic, gullible and poorly educated. The more educated you become, the more you will become a skeptic.

2. University professors are usually unbelievers because they know things unrecognized by average folk that make belief in the Bible a silly thing to have.

3. Religion is a matter of private, personal feelings and should be kept out of debates—political and/or moral—in the public square.

4. Science is the only way to know reality with confidence, or at least it is a vastly superior way of knowing reality than other approaches, e.g., religious ones. And science has made belief in God unnecessary.

5. We can know things only through our five senses. If I can see, touch, taste, hear or smell something, then it's real and I can know it. But if I can't sense it in one of these ways, I can't know it's real and I must settle for a blind, arbitrary choice to believe in it.

6. If we can't get the experts to agree on something like the existence and nature of God, abortion, or life after death, then we just can't know anything about it.

7. Enlightened people are tolerant, nonjudgmental and compassionate. They are unwilling to impose their views on others. Defensive, unenlightened people are the dogmatic, ugly polar opposites of enlightened folk. (Note: We will refer to each of these statements by their numbers in the pages that follow.)

These ideas are seldom stated this explicitly, but we absorb them daily through conversation and largely through the media. This is not a conspiracy. That would be intentional. It's far worse than that. With genuine exceptions, these ideas have so permeated our society that media folk govern their work by them without having the slightest idea of this fact. How do we erase the impact of these background assumptions on our confidence in God and the Christian worldview?

Here's a four-step procedure that will remove this kind of doubt if you internalize it as a habit through conscious repetition:

Step 1) Spot the activating source (e.g., the evening news, TV show, movie, conversation at work) and be alert while being exposed to it.

Step 2: Explicitly state to yourself exactly the doubt-inducing cultural assumption that lies beneath the surface of the activating source (start with the list of seven above).

Step 3: Challenge and question the truth of the cultural assumption. Is that really true? Doubt the doubt!

Step 4: Replace the cultural assumption with a biblical truth—the correct alternative way of seeing reality—and make it your goal to grow in God-confidence about the alternative.

Unmasking Cultural Myths

Let's unpack these steps. Step 1 directs us to be alert in spotting the specific sources of the background assumption. It is usually a movie, a television show (especially news programs, which have become rumor mills for secularism) or print media. The goal is not to become paranoid or to be unable to enjoy the evening news. But we simply must develop the habit of being on the alert while exposing ourselves to these sorts of input. The seven assumptions above are not exhaustive, but they are pervasive, so a good place to start is to remind ourselves of these as we watch the news or process a movie we have seen.

Step 2 instructs us to identify the specific unspoken background assumptions from the sources specified in step 1. We have already listed seven.

Step 3 reminds us to challenge the truth of these ideas—doubt them, challenge them, call them into question. What is the evidence for and against these claims? Are they always true or are there exceptions? Did we absorb this belief without knowing we had done so? Here's an example: If science says something, then it's quite likely to be true. Science says DNA is the source of our genetic information. If there is a soul, its main job is to go to heaven or hell when one dies. The soul, if it is real, plays no role in the development of the body. That role is filled exclusively by DNA.

Now, in the first sixteen centuries of church history, many Christian thinkers believed that the soul was the source of a person's bodily traits. In contemporary times, a growing number of scientists and related scholars are abandoning the notion that DNA comprehensively accounts for all that makes up a human in favor of a view that is very close to the soul view embraced throughout much of church history. There exists considerable scientific and philosophical evidence for the soul view, and it is important for Christians to understand that the debate over the soul is far from being settled in favor of the mechanistic DNA view. Our purpose in raising this topic is not to address the details of the debate here. We have done that elsewhere.[7] The purpose is to show just how deeply we have absorbed the notion that we should get our view of reality primarily from science and not from the Bible or the history of doctrine in the church.

Unfortunately, we don't have space to refute adequately the seven assumptions identified above (page 48), but a few points can be usefully made here. First, note that in that list of cultural assumptions, statements (4), (5), (6) and (7) are all self-refuting. Something is self-refuting if it sets up criteria that make its own claim false. An example would be the statement, "All English sentences are shorter than three words." In the same way, the claim that science is the only way of knowing reality is itself a knowledge claim that can in no way be tested scientifically. Similarly, there is no way to use our five senses to test whether the claim that the senses are our only sources of knowledge is true. One can clearly cite relevant sensory experiences for testing whether an apple is on a table, but just exactly what sensations could settle the truthfulness of (5)?

Regarding (6), experts do not agree that there has to be expert agreement on a subject before anyone can know who's right. So claim (6) fails by its own standards. Additionally, another reason (6) is clearly false is that experts in a field such as religion or ethics often have emotional baggage and ideological axes to grind, preventing them from dealing fairly with the topic in question. Consider when these people are interviewed in the news. They often skirt certain questions they are asked, and they do not exhibit intellectual honesty in evaluating the view they are against. Finally, people who assert claim (7) are themselves intolerant of people who don't agree with their view of tolerance—for example, of those who are moral absolutists, believers who claim that Christ is the only way or prolife people. In fact, the second sentence of (7) is an "intolerant" statement that contradicts the call to tolerance expressed in the first sentence of (7).

Besides the problem of self-refutation, there are a few other brief points we should make. Point (1) (it is smarter to doubt than to believe things) is intellectually irresponsible because our lives flourish with truth but flounder with falsehoods. If you take the medicine that is truly helpful, you get well. If you take the wrong medicine, the results can be disastrous. And failing to take the right medicine can be just as harmful as or more harmful than taking the wrong medicine. While at an airport, if you fail to go to the right gate (maybe by refusing to go to any gate at all), that's as disastrous as going to the wrong one.

A flourishing life is one that believes more and more truths and fewer and fewer falsehoods as one matures. And a flourishing life can be stopped dead in its tracks by refusing to embrace truths that are available to those who could and should want to know them, every bit as much as believing something false. *The right approach to life is one that hungers to know as many truths as one can and to avoid as many falsehoods as possible.* There is no pride of place given to either of these tasks. However, people who live by statement (1) will end up believing fewer falsehoods than most, but they will also fail to avail themselves of many, many truths that could have helped them in their journey if they had simply refused to be so skeptical, and instead sought truth and the avoidance of error without giving greater weight to the latter as statement number 1 dictates. Following (1) is just too high a price to pay for appearing to others to be fashionably skeptical!

Furthermore, it's a cultural lie that the more educated you become, the more you reject Christianity. A few years ago, University of North Carolina sociologist Christian Smith published what may be the most extensive study to date of the impact of contemporary culture on American evangelicalism. Smith's extensive research led him to conclude that

> self-identified evangelicals have more years of education than fundamentalists, liberals, Roman Catholics, and those who are nonreligious. . . . Of all groups, evangelicals are the least likely to have only a high-school education or less; the nonreligious are the most likely. Furthermore, higher proportions of evangelicals have studied at the graduate-school level than have fundamentalists, liberals, or the nonreligious.[8]

It is important for evangelicals to know the facts that Smith reports because an individual's or a community's confidence is significantly shaped by how they perceive that others perceive them.

Today, we evangelicals perceive that others see us as ignorant and naive, as expressed in statements (1) and (2) above. As a result, we come to believe this of ourselves, with the result that we tend to feel small and less powerful and less educated than secular people. The only way this source of doubt can be overcome is to be exposed to and constantly reminded of the truth of the matter as provided by Smith.

But if Smith is correct, why do we evangelicals feel the way we do? We think the answer is the overwhelming influence that movies, television and the media play in shaping our view of what is real and true, coupled with the fact that these sources overwhelmingly depict the culture as secular and shape it in that direction. Don't we tend to feel that if it's on television (especially television news), then it's real? And, if it's not on television, it's *not* real or important? We may not own that we accept this assertion—and consciously we probably don't. But in all honesty, the truth of this claim influences us at a subconscious level more than we realize. If this weren't true, then why would advertisers pay billions of dollars trying to associate their products with things—such as sexual power—that at a conscious level would be ludicrous? Do you consciously believe that a certain brand of deodorant will make women (or men) drop dead with desire to pursue you? Yet this is exactly the point people unconsciously absorb through repeated exposure to the relevant advertisements. In the same way, people absorb a secular view of the world.

Consider this. In *The Culture of Disbelief,* Yale law professor Stephen Carter notes the following:[9]

- When Hillary Clinton was seen wearing a cross at her husband's inauguration, a well-known television commentator complained that it was inappropriate to display so openly a religious symbol.

- In the mid-1980s secular liberals claimed that Pat Robertson was a dangerous Neanderthal because he believed that God can heal disease. Apparently, if we believe such a thing, we are not supposed to say so.

• In the mid-1980s, civil libertarians expressed the view that religious barriers to certain behaviors, such as divorce, abortion and homosexuality, merely express ideas that only exist in the minds of believers, that is, that are figments of people's imagination.

Stephen Carter correctly concludes that such attitudes conveyed through the media express the conviction that religious ideas are arbitrary, unimportant and irrational, something that rational, informed people would do best to avoid.

If television, movies and the media cause intellectual doubt by presenting a secularized version of society, including a view of the cultural and educational elite as largely secular and the uneducated as largely evangelical, what can one do to remove this source of doubt? We suggest a strategy of defense and offense. First, don't be a passive consumer of entertainment and media input. When you expose yourself to these sources, actively put on your thinking cap, work through the four-step process to filter what you see through the lenses of Scripture and a biblical worldview, and consciously doubt what you receive when you sense that it is undermining your God-confidence. Be active and aggressive about this.

A helpful strategy of offense is to develop a counterculture in which believers are regularly exposed to Christian scholars, sophisticated Christian alternatives to secular ideas, and thoughtful Christian books, magazines and journals. Note, such exposure is not important merely so Christians can come to develop Christian alternatives to secular ideas. *It is not just secular ideas that must be countered. It is the process of secularization itself that must be confronted, including the process of socializing Christians into thinking of themselves as marginalized, weak, gullible, uneducated people.* Thus, even if you are not yourself particularly well-educated, and even if you cannot understand the line of reasoning of articulate Christian scholars and carefully thought-out Christian books, exposure to the very existence of such things can provide you with confidence and remove doubt rooted in cultural background assumptions.

Social historian John Gager demonstrates that even though the early church was a minority movement that faced intellectual and cultural ridicule and marginalization, the early church maintained internal cohesion, a courageous witness and a confident faith thanks in no small measure to the powerful role in the broader Christian community of Christian intellectuals and apologists in the first centuries of the Christian faith.[10] The early church knew who her intellectuals and apologists were, and this gave believers confidence and a feeling of strength. In the same way, we must identify, make, celebrate and utilize our Christian intellectuals as role models. And we need to celebrate the absolutely unequaled history of the intellectual life in the Christian church throughout our history. If there is an alternative community of atheists, Buddhists or anyone else that can rival the rich cultural and intellectual leadership in church history, let someone come forth and demonstrate it. The intellectual life is our heritage as Christians, and it is time to remind ourselves of this.

Dealing with Specific Intellectual Doubts

In contrast to the vague doubts subconsciously absorbed through the perpetrators of secularism's plausibility structure, there is another sort of doubt that is a horse of an entirely different color: a specific intellectual doubt. Such a doubt has two characteristics: the doubting person is clearly aware of it, and he or she can write it down on paper. The doubt is quite precise and explicit. Here are eight steps for removing such doubts and increasing your God-confidence.

Step 1: Approach the issue with the hope that you will find an intellectually satisfying answer. In his study of doubt, Christian Smith reports one Christian who, typical of many, opined: "I do not do anything to try to resolve my doubts, I just live with them. They don't worry me. I have accepted that I am going to have some doubts. Someday, I will find out if I am right or wrong."[11] This defeatist approach—the ostrich approach—is not the one to take. Remember: It is the experience of many believers that when they seek diligently for answers to doubts, they find intellectually satisfying answers. This has surely been our experience. It is highly unlikely that someone in the history of the church or in contemporary times has not dealt with the problem adequately.

Step 2: Be sure the doubt is really intellectual. I (J. P.) once had a roommate who was debilitated by fear that he had committed the unpardonable sin. For weeks I reminded him of the accepted interpretations of what this sin is and of why it was impossible for him to have committed it. But this was to no avail. It wasn't until I approached the source of the doubt as an emotional problem that it was removed. Due to early childhood attachment issues, he felt unloved by and disconnected from people in general and God in particular, and rather than face this head on, he projected his emotional insecurity onto the unpardonable sin as a more manageable center of focus. Here's how to tell if your doubt is not largely intellectual: If you have received an intellectual answer to the doubt that satisfies most other believers, especially those more knowledgeable than you, and it doesn't help you, it's likely that the problem isn't intellectual. In the next chapter we'll look at emotional barriers to God-confidence.

Step 3: If the doubt is sourced in the challenges presented by another person, don't assume he or she has considered fairly the available answers to the issue. You may have a relative, coworker or professor who seems smarter and more knowledgeable than you, and this person may harass you with intimidating, opinionated questions you can't answer. When this happens, don't assume that he (or she) really knows his stuff and his attack is the result of a well-reasoned investigation of the issue. Instead, if this happens and you don't know the answer, do three things. First, if the objection is expressed with a lot of anger, mocking and intimidation, chances are the issue is emotional and not intellectual. Don't allow yourself to internalize the attacker's feelings. Set an emotional boundary and don't take on the responsibility to fix that person's problems. If it really is an intellectual problem, the challenging point is usually made with an honest, inquiring tone.

Second, tell the person that you don't have an answer now but that you will get one for him or her. Then either read up on the topic yourself, or if you feel inadequate, find someone in your church who is able to handle the question and arrange a lunch for the three of you. Third, express this to the questioner: "I am sure you have formulated your viewpoint against Christianity in a fair-minded and intellectually responsible way by studying *both* sides of the issue. Since this is so, tell me, what were the four to five best books you have read that *defend* the Christian answer to your claim? And what were the three or four best arguments *against* your conclusion that you had to address in arriving at your skeptical stance, and how did you answer these arguments?" In our experience, hardly anyone has fairly done this kind of homework. This is especially true for most evolutionists who mock intelligent design theory. Note that this approach both removes the responsibility on you to provide an instant answer and calls the attacker to intellectual honesty.

Step 4: Write your doubt down on paper. Work and rework it until you are satisfied that you have clearly stated your doubt in all its facets. Carry this around with you, especially when you plan to meet other Christians or when you attend church.

Step 5: Doggedly find an answer. Don't give up. Take out your paper (step 4) when you are around someone who might have an answer, and jot down his or her response. Ask your pastors for help; ask them for the name of someone in the congregation who knows about the issue. Ask a librarian or someone at your local Christian bookstore for a book or books on the topic. If there is a Christian high school or college near you, find a teacher or professor who can help, get an appointment with him or her, and take your paper with you.

Step 6: Doubt your doubts. Write down on paper a number of reasons why your doubt isn't that defensible after all. Use these reasons as ongoing self-talk; for example, when the doubt comes up in your mind, train yourself to immediately turn your attention to your doubts about the doubt.

Step 7: Remember that there is a communal dimension to knowledge. There are many things we know, not because they can be proven but because there are several, genuine experts with knowledge about the subject who do know the answers to the question. For example, I used to have questions about the historicity of Moses and other portions of the Old Testament. But I have had neither time nor the desire independently to find specific answers to these questions. Instead, I know that there are hundreds of evangelical Old Testament scholars who are fully aware of the objections and who have solid answers to them. It's impossible to know everything, so we must be willing to rely on other members of the body to help us. This is no different from non-Christians. No one can know everything available in a culture, and we all have to rest secure that there are genuine experts who know, for example, that a certain medicine is safe. Think of how bad it would be if there were no intellectuals available who were solid believers. Fortunately, there are scholars in virtually every academic discipline who are solid evangelicals who know full well the problems in their fields and who are able to answer them to their own satisfaction.

Step 8: Remember that atheists and skeptics have as many doubts as we do or more. When a person is vulnerable and afraid, he or she often projects onto others more power than they actually have and fewer fears than the vulnerable person has. We tend to maximize others and minimize ourselves when we feel weak. Applied to matters of faith, if you are suffering from doubt, it's easy to project onto atheists and other skeptics great confidence in and little doubt about their views.

But this is not a true assessment. For example, atheists are plagued with doubts, and, in fact, many of them pray regularly. They really do repress or suppress the knowledge of God as Paul tells us in Romans 1:18. As comedian Woody Allen noted, "I'm not afraid to die. I just don't want to be there when it happens." On a more serious note and in a moment of rare frankness, atheist philosopher Thomas Nagel admits, "I want atheism to be true and am made uneasy by the fact that some of the most intelligent and well-informed people I know are religious believers. It isn't just that I don't believe in God and, naturally, I hope that I'm right in my belief. It's that I hope there is no God! I don't want there to be a God; I don't want the universe to be like that."[12] Influential young atheist Douglas Coupland discloses this:

> Now—here is my secret: I tell it to you with an openness of heart that I doubt I shall ever achieve again, so I pray that you are in a quiet room as you hear these words. My secret is that I need God—that I am sick and can no longer make it alone. I need God to help me give, because I no longer seem capable of giving; to help me be kind, as I no longer seem capable of kindness; to help me love, as I seem beyond being able to love.[13]

So remember, our critics are not as sure of themselves as they want us to believe. Come to think about it, since they are made in the image of God, that's what we should have expected all along.

A Final Word of Encouragement

As I (J. P.) write this, I recall that earlier today while waiting for a doctor's appointment, I noticed a woman reading a book on the writings of Moses. Curious, I asked her why she was reading the book, and she turned out to be a believer who was taking a class on the Old

Testament. At one point in our conversation, she said something extremely relevant to intellectual doubt. For years, she had read the Bible with a quiet fear that just maybe none of the events recorded had actually happened. She had comforted herself by reading the events as spiritual events that were real—sort of—but whose importance was primarily "spiritual" and to be accepted by pure faith. But when she took a class on the Gospels and now on the Old Testament, she discovered solid evidence that both were historically reliable, that the locations mentioned were real places and that archeology had regularly confirmed scriptural historicity. Then came the clincher. Now, she gushed, she had a newfound confidence that these matters "were *really* real." As a result, her confidence in God and his Word was strengthened as well as her boldness in witnessing.

We Christians need never fear honest questions and inquiry, nor need we ever dread future scientific or historical discoveries. Instead, we should eagerly await them, because in the final analysis and on the basis of many things, including the Bible's track record, truth can only help us in our Christian journey. Who knows? It may even help to set us free![14]

Earlier we mentioned feelings and fears related to intellectual doubts. In the next chapter, we'll explore this affective side of our life further, for these also can become barriers to trusting in God.

> *It is your senses and your imagination that are going to attack
>   belief. Here, as in the New Testament, the conflict is not
>   between faith and reason but between faith and sight. . . .
> Our faith in Christ wavers not so much when real arguments come
>   against it as when it looks improbable—when the whole world
>   takes on the desolate look which really tells us much more about the
>   state of our passions and even our digestion than about reality.*

C. S. LEWIS, "RELIGION: REALITY OR SUBSTITUTE"

Questions for Personal Reflection or Group Discussion

1. At the beginning of the chapter, the authors discussed how various people in contemporary society tend to portray Christians. Can you think of any specific examples of when you have heard Christians being negatively depicted in the media, television, movies or music? Describe these examples. What was your response to them? Did you dismiss them or ignore them? Or did these portrayals make you feel angry or embarrassed?

2. One of the key claims in the chapter is that knowledge is central to Christianity. That is, having faith or God-confidence does not preclude having knowledge. How does this fact enhance your understanding of what it means to have God-confidence?

3. Review the four steps the authors suggest for detecting certain cultural assumptions (on page 49). Have these handy the next time you watch the evening news, take in the latest movie, or listen to the radio, and try out each of the four steps yourself. Or perhaps your small group could do this as a group-discussion exercise. What kinds of biases were you able to detect?

4. Do you happen to have any specific intellectual doubts about a particular Christian belief or teaching in the Bible? Or, have you had any doubts in the past? How have you dealt with these in the past? Try using the eight steps on pages 55-59 to interact with and address these doubts.

3

DEALING WITH THE PAST

Distractions of the Heart

Although God has indeed created us with amazing intellectual capacities (our "head"), he has also designed us as richly affective beings (our "heart"). We engage life with both our intellect *and* our emotions. In the last chapter, we examined the "distractions of the head" that can impede our growth in God-confidence. In this chapter, we'll consider how to handle the "distractions of the heart"—the emotional and relational barriers—that can inhibit increasing our God-confidence. We'll take a closer look within our hearts to see what they may reveal about our readiness to rely on God for the challenging situations of life.

When life is going well, it seems it's much easier to be loving and joyful and peaceful. But when we hit the speed bumps of life, somehow a much different side of our character emerges. Jesus tells us that "Good people bring good things out of the good stored up in their heart, and evil people bring evil things out of the evil stored up in their heart. *For out of the overflow of the heart the mouth speaks*" (Luke 6:45 TNIV, emphasis added). When I'm (Klaus) behind on a project trying to finish up with last-minute touches, I can get a bit short with my wife. I'm into my "on task, stay clear" mode. Can you remember a time when you were a bit short with family or room-mates? Or perhaps someone was a bit short with you and you re-sponded in kind?

A few years ago, while I was at an intersection stopped for a red light, the railroad-crossing signal sounded. Those of us on either side of the railroad were in for a long wait. I happened to look through my rearview mirror and noticed a man in the car behind me. He looked like he was involved in an animated conversation with someone, but looking around, I didn't see anyone else in the car or a cell phone on which he could be speaking. Then I realized he wasn't happy about having to wait. Who knows what the urgency was? Perhaps he was late for a business appointment, or maybe his wife was in labor at the nearby hospital. But in the mirror I was watching him bursting with rage, yelling obscenities nonstop at the top of his lungs. This was an individual whose heart or inner life had formed a readiness to erupt in an angry tirade given certain circumstances. I chuckled—not at him, but at myself.

Years earlier I might have been self-righteously overwhelmed by feelings of contempt for this man's overt display of anger. But now I'm more aware of the dark side of my own heart. So my chuckle was one of identification rather than judgment. God's forgiveness and grace are healing more and more of my self-righteousness. Although I'm far from being out of the woods on this, I am in the process of moving into greater peace inside than ever before, and I'm experienc-ing the joy and freedom that come with it! I'm learning that trusting in God involves a process that engages my *head* and my *heart*.

Wounded Places

Some of us may wonder down deep if God really can be trusted. Oh, we may have already become a member of God's family, having ac-knowledged our sinfulness and received the gift of grace from Jesus our Savior. But, if we're painfully honest, some of us would admit we have a few wounded places within where we really don't feel safe with others, particularly with God.

Edith,[1] now in her early twenties, had experienced significant rejection as a child. She shared her story with Ed Piorek at a ministry conference.

> When I was born I had a twin sister who was stillborn at the same time. I had skeletal formation problems but was otherwise healthy. These problems put a financial strain on my parents. When I was five years old, I was standing outside the kitchen and I heard my father say to my mother, "I'll never understand it. Why did the one with the perfectly formed body die and the one with the deformities live?" I know my father was speaking out of his frustrations with the challenges of caring for me, but nevertheless it really hurt. I've never been able to forget it.[2]

It's amazing how one brief moment of indiscretion can set another person on a profoundly painful downward trajectory. Furthermore, what impact did this comment of rejection have on young Edith's image of God—did she unconsciously believe God was very caring? Probably not. Ed was able to help her begin to move beyond the hurt and disappointment caused by her earthly father and begin to sense her heavenly Father's love for her. She responded well to Ed's counsel and took a courageous step that launched her into a healing process on both fronts: she poured her heart out openly to God, sharing the deep wound, and forgave her earthly father for that hurtful comment.

At first glance, the emotional and relational aspects of our lives may seem a bit peripheral to a life of God-confidence. Consider what hindered George from praying for others until much later in his adult years. He realized there was a problem when he joined a group to pray for someone and "no words would come out, I just locked up! I was able to pray privately to God . . . but I couldn't pray out loud."³ This happened a number of times, and George finally fell away from church attendance because of the "doubt, shame and guilt" he felt. He eventually came back and got involved in the church's ministry to the poor. After one Sunday service, George was prompted to receive prayer for his back pain. Even after five surgeries, the pain continued. "I thought I'd give it a shot, after 12 years of intense back pain, I actually called the pain my 'Friend.' I didn't expect much because my prayers were ineffective." God healed his back. And later on, God healed his heart.

A memory came back to George, of a family trip to California when he was six years old. He had remembered it as a trip for his birthday, but it was actually a family visit to be with his dying grandfather. Finally the dots began to connect regarding the root of his prayer problem. His mother had asked him to pray for his grandfather, that God might heal him. "He died that night and when I awoke in the morning he was gone and my birthday was very sad. This had been buried deep for all these years and actually caused a fear of killing anyone I'd pray for." Sometimes it's the case that our lack of God-confidence will relate to false beliefs that stem from earlier experiences. That's why we've devoted a whole chapter to exploring this arena of our inner lives to discern any barriers that might be preventing us from gaining greater reliance on God. Furthermore, these insights might be helpful to those with whom you are ministering.

The Power of Emotions

Some people claim that they don't have an emotional bone in their bodies—they tend to think they rely solely on their intellect. But in reality, we all have powerful emotions that control our actions much more than we realize (remember the guy's tirade while waiting for the train?). The word *emotion* conveys the idea itself: e-motion—emotions *move* us. The more we take notice of our emotional states, and move into healthier emotional places, the more we can be guided by God toward the good and away from foolish and sinful actions.

Life fundamentally consists of *two basic movements:* either we're moving *toward* God, or we're moving *away* from him—there's no neutral zone or middle ground. We all move in one or the other direction. So, if we're unaware of this basic truth and unaware which way our heart is moving us, then for most of the hours of our day and week we'll default to the "away zone." Therefore, a fundamental life skill for all believers is learning how to discern the subtle ways our heart moves us in either direction. Deepening our trust in God requires us to be aware of how our emotional life affects our walk with God. We'll start off by looking at what the Bible teaches about our heart and our desires.

Follow Your Desires or Ignore Them?

Throughout the Old Testament, the term "heart" (Hebrew, *lēb*) represents the self, including thoughts, feelings and the will (e.g., Psalm 22:26; 1 Kings 3:12; Exodus 36:2). In this context, "heart" can be interchangeable with "soul" (Hebrew, *nephesh,* e.g., Joshua 22:5; 1 Samuel 2:35).[4] Usually the New Testament follows this usage for *heart* (Greek, *kardia*). For example, in Acts 14:17, "you" parallels the use of "heart": "[God] provides you with plenty of food and fills your hearts with joy" (see also Luke 21:34; 2 Corinthians 5:12). Occasionally it is used in parallel with "mind" (Greek, *nous,* e.g., 2 Corinthians 3:14-15).[5] Yet on a few occasions the Greek term *kardia* (heart) refers specifically just to our emotional life (e.g., Philippians 4:7). For example, in the upper room Jesus acknowledged the grief in the disciples' hearts (John 16:6, 22), but he desired that they not be troubled in heart (John 14:1, 27). Jesus predicted that when he would see them after his resurrection their hearts would be joyful (John 16:22). That's how we use the word today. After participating in a good Bible study, someone might say, "That truth not only reached my head (my intellect), but it also touched my heart (connected at a deep level affectively)."

Yet when talking about the subject of desires and emotions, Christians can be a bit nervous. The unstated reasoning goes like this: If there's something I really want to do, it's probably sinful. Of course, this could be true in some cases—but not for everything we want to do. Bruce Waltke, professor emeritus of Old Testament studies at Regent College, reminds us that in seeking to know what pleases God, we should actually listen to our desires: "One way I know God's will is by the desires of my heart. When God is in control of your life, He is also in control of your desires. The things you long for in your heart are put there by the Holy Spirit."[6] How else could King David say, "Will [God] not bring to fruition my salvation and grant me my every desire?" (2 Samuel 23:5).

Desires and affections are part and parcel of being human. The Spirit works in our feelings and desires:

- Matthew 20:32-34: Moved with compassion, Jesus healed the two blind men.

- Luke 22:59-62: Peter wept bitterly after denying Jesus three times.

- 2 Corinthians 1:3-4: God comforts us in our pain; later we comfort others with the same comfort.

Key "fruit" that the Spirit yields in our lives (Galatians 5:22-23) involves significant emotional aspects, such as love (Romans 12:9-10), joy (Acts 13:52) and peace (Philippians 4:6-7). Furthermore, God actually desires to fulfill our desires, as King David teaches.

> Trust in the LORD and do good;
>> dwell in the land and enjoy safe pasture.
> *Delight yourself in the LORD*
>> *and he will give you the desires of your heart.*

Commit your way to the LORD;
>trust in him and he will do this:
He will make your righteousness shine like the dawn,
>the justice of your cause like the noonday sun.

Be still before the LORD and wait patiently for him;
>do not fret when men succeed in their ways,
>when they carry out their wicked schemes.

Refrain from anger and turn from wrath;
>do not fret—it leads only to evil.
(Psalm 37:3-8, emphasis added)

C. S. Lewis believed that desires played an important part in the Christian life and thought that most Christians settled for far too little in fulfilling their desires. In his book *The Weight of Glory and Other Addresses* he writes:

The New Testament has lots to say about self-denial, but not about self-denial as an end in itself. We are told to deny ourselves and to take up our crosses in order that we may follow Christ; and nearly every description of what we shall ultimately find if we do so contains *an appeal to desire*. If there lurks in most modern minds the notion that to desire our own good and earnestly to hope for the enjoyment of it as a bad thing, I submit that this notion has crept in from Kant and the Stoics and is no part of the Christian faith. Indeed, if we consider the unblushing promises of reward and the staggering nature of the rewards promised in the Gospels, it would seem that *Our Lord finds our desires not too strong, but too weak*. We are half-hearted creatures, fooling about with drink and sex and ambition when infinite joy is offered us, like an ignorant child who wants to go on making mud pies in a slum because he cannot imagine what is meant by the offer of a holiday at the sea. *We are far too easily pleased.*[7]

Unfortunately desires and emotions have been given a bad rap by many Christian leaders. Not only have desires been off the conceptual radar screen, but many of us are often clueless about how we really feel and what we really want. That's been my case for most of my life—I'm now fifty-six! But the greatest danger about being unaware of this affective side is that Satan loves to lure us away from God by playing on our desires.

Our Desires: The Target of Temptation

James 1:14 identifies our desires as the point of contact for temptation. "But one is tempted by one's own desire *[epithymia]*, being lured and enticed by it" (NRSV). Other translations interpret *epithymia* as "evil desire" (Holman, CSB, TNIV). A standard Greek lexicon places the majority of the New Testament uses of this term in one of two categories, as emphasized in the following Scriptures.[8] It conveys either a *good* sense (e.g., Philippians 1:23, "I am torn between the two: I *desire* to depart and be with Christ, which is better by far"), or a *bad* or *evil* sense (e.g., Colossians 3:5, "Put to death, therefore, whatever belongs to your earthly nature: sexual immorality, impurity, lust, evil *desires* and greed, which is idolatry"). There's a smaller third category for use in a neutral sense—desires, whether good or bad. This was the predominant secular use (e.g., Mark 4:19, "But the worries of this life, the deceitfulness of wealth and the *desires* for other things come in and choke the word, making it unfruitful").

How should *epithymia* be translated here in James 1:14? It depends on whether James's statement is intended to be a *comprehensive* statement about all kinds of temptation or not. For example, if it is translated as "evil desire" (NIV) as the primary beginning point in the process of every temptation, then how can we account for the temptation of Adam and Eve, before they had sinned and had no evil desire? We'll also need to look elsewhere to explain how Jesus was tempted, since he never had an evil desire, although the Bible teaches he was actually tempted in many ways (Hebrews 5:14). It seems best to understand *epithymia* in a neutral sense (NRSV) as referring to any desire, whether it is good or bad. The other occurrence of *epithymia* in James 4:1 fits that broad range as well.

Thus, either good *or* bad human desire is the beginning point for any temptation. In the case of a bad desire, it usually has its own downward pull toward evil and needs no other push to move into becoming a sinful action. As James explains it, "Then, after desire has conceived, it gives birth to sin; and sin, when it is full-grown, gives birth to death" (James 1:15). But for good desire to lead to sin, another influence of an evil sort is needed. Although God does test believers to *im*prove them and *ap*prove them (cf. James 1:2-4 and James 1:12), God never tempts anyone to do evil: "When tempted, no one should say, 'God is tempting me.' For God cannot be tempted by evil, nor does he tempt anyone" (James 1:13). Another supernatural agent takes that distinctive role, "the tempter" (Matthew 4:3-5; 1 Thessalonians 3:5). Implicit throughout the letter of James is Satan's evil activity, made explicit in James 4:7 ("Resist the devil, and he will flee from you") and in James 3:15 ("of the devil," NIV; "demonic," NASB).

Consider this personal example of movement away from God, being enmeshed in turmoil: Somehow I couldn't stop thinking about it. I was working on a project with another colleague, and our deadline was just thirty days away. It had already been postponed once because of an event beyond our control. I was getting nervous because I don't like missing deadlines; I've got a reputation to keep. I thought we needed to pull out all the stops to get it done soon, but my colleague didn't see it the same way. An imaginary dialogue kept bouncing around my mind trying to justify my point of view. It was like getting sucked into a whirlpool; whenever my mind was free, it just went back to that same issue over and over again. I was obsessing about the matter, and it finally dawned on me that this was not a good thing.

"Lord, what's this about?" In my journal I jotted down the various thoughts that came to mind, hoping I'd get some clarity. I realized I was being overly responsible. We were already doing our best to bring the project to completion. My good desire for being responsible and being on time was the target of the temptation. Mix that in with the busyness of the month of December and I could see that my "controlling" coping strategy was kicking in gear. Once the dots were connected, as I confessed my sin to God, I was overcome by an amazing sense of freedom and relief—no longer was I obsessing about the matter, no whirlpool was sucking me down. I apologized to my colleague, and that cleared the air between us.

Our good desires can easily be used to move us a bit off course, which eventually could lead us into destructive behavior. Satan's purpose is to lead us immediately or eventually away from God. So, when we end up in this kind of disaster, it's a good idea to reflect back on the matter and ask, Was there a good desire or apparent good we hoped for at the starting point of the chain of events? Our reflection involves moving along the chain of events backwards to the beginning, considering the various issues, concerns and motivations related to how it all began. If a good desire or apparent good does not come to mind at first, don't give up. Keep reflecting and usually there'll be a good desire somewhere in the background. Any desire, good or bad, can easily be hijacked for evil. The metaphor actually depicted in James 1:14 is of fishing with alluring bait—being "dragged away and enticed." Temptations don't come with loud sirens going off to warn us—they're usually very subtle. By noticing the specific patterns in our lives that easily lead to disaster, we can become more alert to these temptations of our good desires so we can remain firm and keep moving toward God and not away from him.

Hijacked Emotions

Jesus' temptations at the beginning of his public ministry illustrate how our affective life is open game for Satan's attempts to hijack us (Matthew 4:1-10). Jesus had fasted for forty days in the wilderness. His basic bodily desires were calling out to him. The devil started with the normal desire of hunger as the target: make bread out of these stones. For Jesus, that's a possibility; later in his ministry he fed more than five thousand people with five loaves and two fish (Matthew 14:17). But now is a time for fasting for Jesus. Jesus responded to Satan with Scripture, stating that life is not all about eating, but about depending on God for all our needs (Deuteronomy 8:3).

Because Jesus had mentioned the Word of God, this time the devil quoted Scripture, knowing that Jesus would perk up his ears at that (even Scripture can be used by Satan to tempt us away from God). The devil took Jesus to the pinnacle of the temple and challenged him, "If you are the Son of God, . . . throw yourself down. For it is written . . ." (Matthew 4:6). The passage quoted by Satan is interesting for it first mentions that angels care for God's people (and especially God's anointed). "For he will command his angels concerning you to guard you in all your ways; / they will lift you up in their hands, so that you will not strike your foot against a stone" (Psalm 91:11-12). Wasn't the devil an angel? Did Satan use this passage to place himself in a better light, as a (former) messenger of God? Jesus perhaps pondered the passage and considered its message of God's concern and care. Furthermore, perhaps a secondary temptation involved attracting the temple worshipers to witness this potential miraculous rescue as a public presentation of God's Messiah.

Jesus had lived in thirty years of obscurity. Such a miraculous rescue could jump start his public ministry. Hadn't Jesus come to make God known to Israel? But he didn't take the bait. His special sonship had just been confirmed to him by the Father at his baptism: "And a voice from heaven said, 'This is my Son, whom I love; with him I am well pleased'" (Matthew 3:17). Forcing God's hand in this manner and at this time was not a good idea. It wasn't yet the time for a showy confirmation, through a powerful miracle, that Jesus was God's anointed (as happened later at the raising of Lazarus from the dead, John 11:1-53). Jesus would rest in God's care—what Psalm 91 taught—by patiently waiting for God's timing, both for food and for the miraculous (the first miracle took place soon thereafter, turning water into wine, John 2:11). Flashy pomp and circumstance was not the way to launch his public ministry.

Finally, the devil took Jesus to a mountain to give him a vision of the glory of all the kingdoms of the world. All this would be Jesus' if he'd bow down and worship the devil. Perhaps Satan was luring Jesus to become the King sooner than later, taking a shortcut without having to go to the cross. But Jesus would have probably recognized that route to be bad theology since the sin issue still had to be addressed. Furthermore, it's difficult to imagine that Jesus actually trusted that this "used car salesman" would ever deliver on any promises. Jesus was convinced that Satan was a liar from the beginning (John 8:44). So perhaps Satan was up to something more devilish; there was a devious and subtle aspect to this promise of grandeur.

Consider again Satan's words, "if you will bow down and worship me" (Matthew 4:9). Wouldn't this be an offensive and insulting comment to Jesus, who is himself God? Since Jesus received worship during his incarnation (Matthew 14:33; 28:17; Luke 24:52; John 9:38; 20:28), why should Jesus' response to Satan be about the Father only? "Jesus said to him, 'Away from me, Satan! For it is written: 'Worship the Lord your God, and serve him only'" (Matthew 4:10). Jesus often referred to himself in the third person, such as in the many Son of Man sayings (e.g., "Jesus replied, 'Foxes have holes and birds of the air have nests, but the Son of Man has no place to lay his head,'" Matthew 8:20). So when Jesus quoted from Deuteronomy 6:13 in Matthew 4:10, "Worship the Lord your God, and serve him only," was Jesus also pointing to himself, indicating that Satan should be the one worshiping Jesus, rather than the other way around?

Satan is a master at temptation. As recorded in the Old Testament, he was able to stir up Moses, who was then disqualified from entering the Promised Land, by tempting him to sin and anger (Numbers 20:8-13; Psalm 106:32-33). Who hasn't become overwhelmed by anger and done things they regretted later? Perhaps Satan had the same goal in mind for Jesus. But Jesus recognized his ploy and didn't permit this arrogant insult by Satan to stir up sinful anger. Yet Jesus' response seems to include a measure of controlled irritation, "Away from me, Satan!" (Matthew 4:10). This was Jesus' first command recorded in Matthew's Gospel, and the first use of *Satan* (adversary) in the Gospels. Isn't it possible that behind his Deuteronomy 6:13 quotation Jesus was also pointing to his own deity (You should be worshiping me! [Matthew 4:10]). When Satan left, the Father sent angels to minister to him (i.e., bring him food). So the Father did send angels to care for him (Matthew 4:11, thus actually demonstrating Psalm 91:11 in Jesus' life, related to temptation number two) and miraculously provided food to eat (related to temptation number one, as an angel had done for Elijah, 1 Kings 19:5-8). The Father ministered to the very issues that Satan had raised in these first two temptations.

Satan uses *any* means, ethical or unethical, to distract us from trusting in God, drawing us away to trust in ourselves by moving us into fear, into anger, into pride. Sadly, it works most of the time. Like Peter in the storm walking on the water, we lose our focus on Jesus; we let our dark emotions overwhelm us and we start sinking. Even our good desires are the target for temptation. But we're also susceptible to retreating into sinful coping strategies. As I mentioned, my own downward spiral of thoughts was coaxed along by my need to control the situation—a coping strategy I had learned long ago. Somehow I didn't feel safe in that situation, and my overreaction was to control. What was helpful in this situation? First, becoming aware of the downward spiral in my self-talk; then labeling it as not healthy; and, finally, asking God to help me gain insight as to the source of the problem. We don't need to be on Satan's leash. We can become more alert to the fact that our desires do play a key role in what we do.

Going Deeper into the Father's Love

We've both realized that even though we seek to do our best as parents (our children are now grown), our love for our children will always fall short of the ideal standard of God's unconditional love. We're both imperfect persons, so we will also be imperfect parents. And that also applies to our own parents. Some of the wounded places in our hearts resulted from growing up in homes with imperfect parents. No matter how good our parents were or how thoughtless at times—in extreme cases some parents may have been regularly abusive—human beings this side of heaven can never give us a continual flow of unconditional love. And so, in some degree, we all carry with us some deep wounds related to our growing-up years.

Furthermore, our initial perception of God is largely formed by our interaction with our parents and other early caregivers. As children, to be safe, we developed ways of coping with our imperfect parents. And due to these varied challenging experiences in our childhood, perhaps some of us may wonder how safe God really is. Furthermore, these childhood strategies to be safe become now in adulthood barriers for us in our relationship with God since we tend to rely on our own limited powers to fix the problem, to be safe, rather than to rely on the Father's help and his unconditional love. Alluding to the parable of the prodigal son, Henri Nouwen laments, "I am the prodigal son every time I search for unconditional love where it cannot be found. Why do I keep ignoring the place of true love and persist in looking for it elsewhere? Why do I keep leaving home where I am called a child of God, the Beloved of the Father?"[9]

Of course as long as we continue our lives on this earth, we acquire additional "heart wounds" through experiences at school, in the dog-eat-dog climate of the work world, and even through our involvement and ministries at church. Yet our good Heavenly Father pursues us to break through these defenses we have constructed to keep ourselves safe, so that the Father can touch our hearts with his forever love. As someone has well said, "Heaven is one continual hug."

Floyd McClung, former president of Youth With A Mission, was teaching about God's "Father heart" at a conference. Following one of the sessions, a shy teenage girl waited for him. Her initial question was not the pressing concern. As Floyd waited, she sat down beside him "in the small, crowded auditorium and whispered in my ear, 'Can I cry on your shoulder?' Sure."[10] When she was young, her father had died, and she had no daddy to comfort her and listen to her joys and sorrows. Floyd continues, "She cried unashamedly on my shoulder, then we talked to our Father in heaven. Together we asked him to heal the hurt and fill the empty space in her life."[11]

Jesus would often spend time alone, fellowshiping with and praying to the Father, seeking and enjoying that special relationship (Mark 1:35). Jesus always began his prayers with "Abba," a more personal and intimate form of address to the Father. New Testament scholar Scot McKnight explains,

> Jesus is decidedly lopsided when it comes to names for God: *every prayer* of Jesus recorded in the Gospels begins with "*Abba*, Father" except the famous "My God, my God, why have you forsaken me?" utterance from the cross. . . . What Jesus wants to evoke with the name *Abba* is God's unconditional, unlimited, and unwavering love for his people. In this name for God we are standing face-to-face with the very presence of spiritual formation: God loves us and we are his children.[12]

And we, who are in Christ, have the same privilege to come to God with this same term of endearment and familiarity:

For you did not receive a spirit that makes you a slave again to fear, but you received the Spirit of sonship. And by him we cry, "*Abba*, Father." (Romans 8:15, emphasis added)

Because you are sons, God sent the Spirit of his Son into our hearts, the Spirit who calls out, "*Abba*, Father." (Galatians 4:6, emphasis added)

New Testament scholar Douglas Moo states that "intimacy with God is certainly suggested by *abba* (and by *pater* [Greek, Father] as well)."[13] Martin Luther offered these comforting comments on the Galatians 4:6 verse:

This is but a little word, and yet notwithstanding it comprehends all things. The mouth speaks not, but the affection of the heart speaks after this manner: Although I be oppressed with anguish and terror on every side, and seem to be forsaken and utterly cast away from your presence, yet am I your child, and you are my Father for Christ's sake: I am beloved, because of the Beloved.[14]

Whether we are conscious of it or not, from the white-collared stockbroker on Wall Street to the Lost Boys of Sudan, all of us yearn for the hug of eternal comfort, for that embrace of unconditional love. Since God is our Father, we can reach up our hands and "cry, '*Abba*, Father'" (Romans 8:15).

Becoming Aware of Our Hidden Places

Is growing deeper in our trust with God really tied up with being more aware of our inner, emotional life? Why should we bother? Because God values our deepest honesty about ourselves. Consider David's psalm of confession: "Surely you desire truth in the inner parts; you teach me wisdom in the *inmost place*" (Psalm 51:6, emphasis added). The term translated "inmost place" (Hebrew, *satum*) typically appears in a different context, that of "'plugging up' available water sources (wells, springs, channels) to prevent their use by another party"[15] (e.g., Genesis 26:15, 18; 2 Kings 3:19, 25; 2 Chronicles 32:3-4, 30). Ezekiel 28:3 and Daniel 8:26 also use the word for "hiding away." Gerald Wilson makes the connection to Psalm 51:6: "God seeks open access to those parts of our lives that we choose to keep deeply hidden within our inner world."[16] To ignore God's invitation to be open to his searching gaze would indicate a willful resistance to his loving embrace in the deep parts of our lives.

Sadly, we're often clueless about our own foibles, blind spots and vices (Jeremiah 17:9). We tend to focus on the speck of sawdust in another's eye, but we can't see the huge plank jutting out of our own (Matthew 7:3-5)! It's not natural to look within, to attend to our own limitations, weaknesses and sins. Yet we never need to do this alone, in our own power; we can invite God into this inner search. David the psalmist prays, "Examine me, God, and know my mind; probe me and know my anxieties [sarappay]. / See if you can find in me the way of idolatry and guide me in the age-old way" (Psalm 139:23-24).[17] We may want to hide within, but if we want to deepen our walk with God and develop greater trust in him, we can be assured of God's help. God promises his divine promptings within, particularly as we immerse ourselves in his Word.

> For the word of God is living and active. Sharper than any double-edged sword, it penetrates even to dividing soul and spirit, joints and marrow; it judges the thoughts and attitudes of the heart. Nothing in all creation is hidden from God's sight. Everything is uncovered and laid bare before the eyes of him to whom we must give account. (Hebrews 4:12-13)

Jack wanted greater intimacy with God; his small group always encouraged him along these lines. But Jack wasn't yet free to talk at a heart level; he was more comfortable talking from his head. He'd rather share his thoughts and opinions than his own feelings. He just never brought them up. When it was his turn to talk, he'd often change the topic of conversation.

> Then one night [Jack] confessed how lonely he was, but at the same time how afraid he was of having others know him inside. The group grew closer to him, as they could feel his heart, and they had a great empathy for him. A marvelous thing happened. He began to sense the presence of both God and others within. He was no longer blocking people out. His confession began the process of repair.[18]

Moving into a healthier emotional life is an important part of the journey of growing deeper with God.

Becoming Healthy Within

Jamey was desperate. For two years his stomach bothered him. All the medical tests he'd undergone had offered no help. He happened to notice that his stomach problems increased whenever his parents visited him. Jamey shared this history with Chuck Kraft, whom he'd sought out for counsel and prayer. Chuck discerned that the problem was related to Jamey's relationship with his parents. Initially Jamey deflected that idea. He appreciated how his dad had been his coach in Little League and had been at his other sports events throughout his schooling. Chuck asked him if he had any stomach problems during those years. After a little reflection, perhaps by divine prompting, this memory suddenly appeared: "Though it wasn't as intense then as it is now, I remember feeling a knot in my stomach before every game, especially when my dad was present."[19]

Further probing revealed that Jamey felt his father was never satisfied with his accomplishments in sports or studies. He actually had felt a sense of terror that he might fail. On his wedding day, he had had the same feeling of terror, and then also at the births of his three children. Furthermore, he realized that whenever he got anxious about his wife's reactions to his plans, his stomach got upset as well. Together, Jamey and Chuck discerned that much of the source of this came from Jamey's father's own early life journey. His dad had often failed at what he tried, and when he succeeded, he never received any recognition. So Jamey's dad had wanted his son to succeed, but no compliments ever came Jamey's way. Rarely did Jamey fail, but when he did, he got the brunt of his dad's anger.

Jamey realized his dad was also a victim, and that brought out his compassion for his dad. Chuck led him in a prayer of forgiveness of his dad. He could now admit his anger against God. The key to Jamey's healing was in opening his heart before God, responding to God's presence through these hurtful memories of the past. Jamey was able to picture Jesus with him in each event, and slowly his stomach pains grew less and less. As Jamey took all this to prayer, God brought him peace and began a healing process in both his emotions and his body.

Sensing Jesus' closeness can become a powerful experience. This happened to my (Klaus's) wife, Beth, during a time of loneliness. Taking risks is not her forte. On one occasion, it seemed to Beth that her friends were willing to step out of their comfort zones regarding new ways of seeking God, while Beth, overcome with fear, was being left behind. That's how she felt, but that wasn't true. Then one afternoon as she was in prayer, in her mind she saw a picture of friends skating on a frozen lake and moving farther away while she stood on the bank, afraid to step out on it. But then she sensed light and warmth coming from behind. She turned around and saw Jesus standing by a barrel with a roaring fire going. He was smiling at her and said, "I won't leave you till you're ready, and I'll go with you." What she had imagined about friends skating away was really friends just skating around in circles nearby. From this experience she took away the comfort of Jesus' presence—that he was near and would not leave her.

I rarely write poetry, but when I do, it's amazing to me how emotionally rich poems can be and what healing occurs in the process of writing. I wrote the following poem as a plea and prayer to Jesus during a time of personal need. And as I wrote, I sensed Jesus' love and presence. Perhaps it may help direct your heart to a deep place that can be touched by Jesus.

Comfort Me, O Sweet Jesus

The little one is crying, Sorrow burdens his heart,
Unmet needs upset his soul, He cries and falls apart.
O Jesus, my heart aches, And I'm just a little one,
I can't bear the pain inside, I feel so all alone.

Jesus, were you there? To know about my pain?
Or were you elsewhere, With more important things?
O little one, I was grieved, And was sad to see your tears,
I was there to carry your pain, Yes, I was very near.

O little one, come to me, Let your tears freely flow,
Crawl up in my lap, Know you're never alone!
O Jesus, help me share my fears, I do feel all alone.
Let me sense your Presence deeply, Comfort these pains
    in my soul.

O little one, I'm right here, Sitting right beside.
Tell Me what you wish, There's no need to hide.
Comfort me, O sweet Jesus, Touch the places that still throb,
Soothe me with your peace and joy, Hold me in your arms
    of love.

Only infinite divine love can touch our deep places of sorrow. Only infinite divine love can heal our wounds and lift us up. Living more and more in divine love is an important and normal part of God's program for us.

Wholeness Within Minimizes Opportunities for Satan

While pastor Ed Piorek was speaking at a conference, he sensed that someone in attendance was about to enter into an adulterous relationship. At the end of the session, rather than let it go as just another fleeting thought, he shared this concern with the audience and mentioned he would be available for a private conversation. Later that afternoon, "a young man came up to me and whispered in my ear, 'I am the one you were talking about.'"[20] Moving to a private location, Gerald shared his story. Gerald had recently married April, a divorced woman with four children, and she was a bit older than Gerald. The courtship went well, but managing a household with four children was not what he anticipated. It was straining his emotional and even sexual ties with April. Gerald felt abandoned. As time went on, Gerald grew emotionally attached to a woman at work who always had a listening ear for him. Their relationship had progressed to the point that Gerald was planning to meet with her at a hotel that very afternoon. "Your word earlier seems to have stopped me in my tracks."[21]

Ed thought there was a deeper issue involved than just his wife's apparent distance. Through further prompting, Gerald revealed that his father had abandoned him at birth. What Gerald was really seeking was the missing love of his father, which wouldn't be found in the arms of another woman. Ed presented the metaphor of the prodigal son and suggested that Gerald "needed to run for the arms of his Father in heaven."[22] Gerald heard the words, but they didn't hit home, so Ed asked,

"Do you love those four boys who now call you father?"

"Oh yes!" he replied.

"How do you think they would feel if you go through with this and break up their home?"

"They would feel abandoned," he said, tears forming in his eyes.

"The way you felt when your father abandoned you?" He began to sob.[23]

Ed drew the parallel that Gerald's heavenly Father felt the same way about Gerald as he was now feeling for those four children. God loved him very much and cared about his feelings of abandonment. In that moment, God's love flooded Gerald's heart, relieving the pain of his sense of abandonment. He began to find the love he was searching for, and he didn't keep that hotel appointment. The moral of the story is, if we don't address the deep needs of our heart, we become the walking wounded and very susceptible to being led down destructive paths.

When Jesus announced to his disciples the first prediction of his coming suffering and death, Peter was not very pleased, and he gave Jesus a piece of his mind. "Peter took him aside and began to rebuke him. 'Never, Lord!' he said. 'This shall never happen to you!'" (Matthew 16:22). We learn that Peter's sinful and negative reaction was not only energized by his concerns, but also stirred up by Satan himself: "Jesus turned and said to Peter, 'Get behind me, Satan! You are a stumbling block to me; you do not have in mind the things of God, but the things of men'" (Matthew 16:23).

Much later in the story, consider the interaction between Jesus and Peter at the Last Supper, as Jesus was anticipating his suffering to come. Peter's prideful boasting of his faithfulness to Jesus prevented him from hearing Jesus' warning about Satan and Jesus' encouraging comment that Jesus had already prayed for him (Luke 22:31-34). "But [Peter] replied, 'Lord, I am ready to go with you to prison and to death'" (Luke 22:33). Flash forward to the trials of Jesus when Peter was in the courtyard, warming himself around the fire. When he was accused of being associated with Jesus, Peter's fears overwhelmed him. Peter's bravado evaporated, and he denied his Lord. These fears distracted him from trusting in Jesus, just as his fear of the waves while walking on the water had distracted him before (Matthew 14:28-31).

Early on, most of us learned that when going through times of fear, we can only trust in ourselves. These old coping strategies are still alive and well in our adulthood. But we also need to become more aware of possible demonic involvement, as was the case in these episodes with Peter. Indeed, Scripture teaches that our patterns of sinful anger may provide an open gate for regular demonic harassment. "'In your anger do not sin': Do not let the sun go down while you are still angry, and do not give the devil a *foothold*" (Ephesians 4:26-27, emphasis added). New Testament professor Clint Arnold explains,

> The most natural way to interpret the use of *topos* (foothold) in Ephesians 4:27 is the idea of inhabitable space. Paul is thus calling these believers to vigilance and moral purity so that they do not relinquish a base of operation to demonic spirits. . . . When [Paul] cautions them about surrendering space to the devil, he is warning them against allowing the devil (or a demonic spirit) to exert a domineering influence in an area of their lives. For a Christian to nurture anger, for example, may grant a demonic spirit inhabitable space.[24]

Of course, Christians can never be demon-possessed or be completely in Satan's control, but when we give Satan a foothold through our sin habits, he can influence us toward continuing or greater evil. Strange as it may seem, we actually may be giving room for increased demonic influence in our lives when we persist in patterns of sinfulness—whether we're clueless about our sinful actions or not. As a part of the process in which God tenderizes our heart to manifest more and more of the fruit of the Holy Spirit, we'll need to battle Satan's various footholds in our lives by attending to our feelings and reactions.

Help for Inner Wholeness

How can we affirm and welcome the affective side of our life and be receptive to movements *toward* God while being alert to being distracted *away* from God through our affections? Recognizing the value and critical role our desires play is an important step forward. Since all humans tend to act based on the strongest desire at the time, labeling all our desires as only "selfish" or "evil" evidences a lack of trust in God. Of course we must become alert to moments when Satan wishes to hijack us by luring us away from God through our desires. But God's power is greater, as Bruce Waltke notes,

> Christians seem to be afraid of talking about the desires of the heart, for fear they will be led astray by Satan, the deceiver. But God is greater than Satan, and if God is controlling your mind, and if you are in communication with Him through Scripture and prayer, then you can trust your conscience to warn you when you begin to step out of line. You can rely on the desires of your heart, because God is in control of them.[25]

Once we become aware of past inner wounds and the persons who were responsible for them, it's important at some point in the process to forgive those who have wounded us. One may also need to work through emotions of anger or a sense of injustice. When Jamey realized that his father was a victim himself from his own early life, his heart expressed compassion for his dad, which made the forgiving process a bit easier. As we bring the matter before God in prayer, we can be honest about our feelings to those responsible, as well as how it seemed that God was distant. God invites our honesty, as Psalm 51:6 teaches. Some of the psalms are fairly bold in their honesty, expressing what some might even consider disrespect to God (e.g., Psalm 39:10-13; 44:9-26). But God is never threatened by frank conversation with him; that's one of his purposes for including these audacious psalms in his Bible.

One of the consequences of dealing with our inner wounds on our own is that we remain trapped by the first ways we developed for coping. For example, we may have used withdrawal within to avoid further pain, outbursts of anger to protect ourselves, being overly orderly and sweating all the details to make sure our environment is controlled and safe. Yet these coping strategies eventually become in adulthood bad habits of compulsion that imprison us. They feel very comfortable, but we aren't really free to live without them or to develop more effective ways of responding to difficulty or challenges. Furthermore, we easily become influenced by Satan to hurt and sin against others. Ultimately, it will be helpful to discern what's driving our actions or reactions, as it was with Gerald, who was seeking love without abandonment through an adulterous relationship. Additionally, we'll need to be open and honest with ourselves and with God to recognize our sinful actions, and repent.

Chuck Kraft uses a helpful analogy depicting Satan's attraction to our sinful habits: *"Demons are like rats and rats go for 'garbage.'"*[26] *Garbage* represents our emotional wounds and spiritual damage, and the resultant coping strategies. The major problem is not the rats but the garbage. We need to take out the garbage. We invite God into our wounded places to bring his love and healing. And, as we confess our sinful habits and, through repentance and spiritual disciplines, these sinful patterns diminish, then Satan's opportunity to influence us becomes much more negligible. Resisting Satan without addressing the garbage will only bring short-term relief.

Largely due to our Western culture, we tend to live life alone, as individuals. But we can't move into healthy places by ourselves, relying on our own limited powers. We need relationships and community to bring us out. It was largely through dysfunctional community that we developed these wounds, and it will only be through healthy community, empowered by God, that healing can take place.[27] We need to invite trusted others to help us notice, monitor, and begin to limit and defeat these sinful reaction patterns so we can grow more and more into the settled rootedness of Jesus' inner life.[28]

A special case of need may be with some adults whose parents divorced during their childhood years. Based on her study of 1,500 young adults aged eighteen to thirty-five (four-year, national survey), Elizabeth Marquardt suggests there is some good news and some bad news. "Some of these adults turned to God and faith and the church as a home away from home, as a father they never had, in search of answers and truth they couldn't find in their families. Thirty-eight percent of the grown children of divorce agreed with the statement, *God became the father or parent I never had in real life*."[29] But others have turned away from God. "They are much less religious overall than their peers who grew up with married parents. They are 14 percent less likely to be a member of a house of worship and also about 14 percent less likely to say that they are very or fairly religious. They're more likely to agree with the statement, *I believe I can find ultimate truths without help from religion*."[30]

Yet no situation is beyond hope and change, for "all things are possible with God" (Mark 10:27). Jesus tells us that God is like a very generous father who gives liberally: "Which of you fathers, if your son asks for a fish, will give him a snake instead? Or if he asks for an egg, will give him a scorpion? If you then, though you are evil, know how to give good gifts to your children, how much more will your Father in heaven give the Holy Spirit to those who ask him!" (Luke 11:11-13). Darrell Bock notes,

> The specific gift Luke has in mind is the Holy Spirit. Since the prayer comes from a disciple, the request is for God's presence, guidance and intimacy. . . . The one who walks with God should be bold and diligent in asking for such benefits. As such, the passage is not simply a blank-check request, but a blank-check request for the necessities of the spiritual life, such

as those mentioned in the Lord's Prayer and those related to spiritual well-being. . . . The illustration is designed to encourage the disciples to ask boldly. In short, ask—and expect God to answer.[31]

For example, David in the Old Testament looked to God during a desperate time after he had fled from King Saul. A band of warriors had gathered around David. But on one occasion, they were about to stone him because the city they were living in had been looted and burned while they were away, and their wives and children had been kidnapped. The Scripture says, David "found strength in the LORD his God" (1 Samuel 30:6).

Do we know and yearn for the comfort the Father can bring to our wounded souls? While on a skiing trip with his family, James Dobson, the founder of the international ministry Focus on the Family, had already got his family off to the slopes, and he was taking the shuttle by himself to join the family. It had not been an easy morning, he shares, "Maybe it will make other families feel a lot better to know that the Dobsons have nerve-wracking days like that."[32] While in this blue funk, he noticed one girl in her late teens standing apart, also waiting for the shuttle truck. He recognized the distinctive evidence of mental retardation, obvious to Dobson since he had worked for many years with developmentally disabled individuals. Empathy overwhelmed his heart, yet he noticed the other skiers—"young, attractive, beautifully outfitted"—distancing themselves from her. She just stood there, gazing up the mountain, repeating the word "Whomever!" over and over again. Everyone got on the flatbed truck. She stood in the center of the truck isolated by the other skiers, except for a big man, who turned out to be her father. Dobson continues,

It was at this point that this man with the kind face did something I will never forget. He walked over to his daughter and wrapped his arms around her. He put his big hand on the back of her head and gently pressed it to his chest. Then he looked down at her lovingly and said, "Yeah, babe. Whomever."[33]

This moving demonstration of love touched Dobson. The message he got from this father was,

Yes, it's true. My daughter is retarded. We can't hide that fact. She is very limited in ability. She won't sing the songs. She won't write the books. In fact, she's already out of school. We've done the best we could for her. But I want you all to know something. This young lady is my girl, and I love her. She's the whole world to me. And I'm not ashamed to be identified with her. "Yeah, babe. Whomever!"[34]

And so does our heavenly Father love us, wrapping his strong arms around us tenderly to embrace and hold us dearly. We must not let any lies of Satan take that fact away.

Yes, we're much more than cognitive beings. There's a significant and rich affective side to being human. God's design is that our good desires enrich and enhance how we live. Sadly, in some faith traditions, feelings and desires have been devalued and deemphasized. In our affective life we can rise to great heights and sink to dark depths. It will be helpful to uncover our past emotional wounds that may hinder our capacity to trust in God and to trust in others. Yet God is safe. But each of us will need to learn that important theological truth experientially, through our own journey of God-confidence. Perhaps God has been bringing to mind an area for further reflection in prayer before him. Consider using one of the suggested ways treated in this chapter as a helpful action point.

◆ ◆ ◆

We now have completed part one of the book, having developed a fuller understanding of the concept of faith itself, as well as addressing some of the barriers or distractions to growing in our trust in God. In part two, we'll focus on increasing our expectations of God, building a case for how our God-confidence can grow. To lead us off in that direction, in the next chapter, we must look at Jesus' teaching about faith, and ponder the amazing promises he offers each believer.

> *[Faith] flows from the heart, the center of the person,*
> *the prefunctional root out of which both the intellectual*
> *and the emotional branches grow.*
>
> PETER KREEFT, *BACK TO VIRTUE*

Questions for Personal Reflection or Group Discussion

1. Do you agree or disagree with the claim that our "heart"—the affective side of our being—influences our confidence in God? Do you agree or disagree with the authors that there are only two inner movements of the heart in relation to God—either movement toward God or movement away from God—and no neutral ground? Why or why not?

2. Think reflectively over your life. Which seasons or occasions in your life would you place in the category of movements *toward* God? Which seasons or occasions in your life would you place in the category of movements *away* from God? What particular aspects are the deciding factors for placing a particular season or occasion in one category or the other? How can reviewing these events in your life through the lens of these two concepts change the way you perceive these experiences?

3. Is it possible for you to name two or three of your core desires or yearnings? Can you discern how God may be working in and

through these desires? Can you detect ways in which Satan could possibly use these desires to distract you away from God? Is it possible for you to name one or two of your coping strategies from your childhood that may now get in the way of trusting more in God?

4. How comfortable are you with exploring your emotions and your inner life? How easy or difficult is it for you to share your faults and weaknesses openly and honestly with others?

PART TWO

EXPANDING EXPECTATIONS
FOR OUR FAITH IN GOD

4

MAKING SENSE OF JESUS'
INCREDIBLE PROMISES

What is the *normal* Christian life? In light of our identity as Christian believers, as followers of Christ, what should we expect our spiritual lives to be like? When we pause to consider whether we are living the *normal* Christian life, we probably answer with both a no and a yes. On one hand, we do *not* believe that we are living the normal Christian life since we know, at least on some level, that there is more to life than what our current spiritual journey includes. On the other hand, we may need to admit that all of the decisions and judgments we make between what is right and what is wrong are based on our current beliefs, character and practice. In this sense, we actually *do* assume that our spiritual journey *is* the normal Christian life. Doesn't this assumption seem true for most believers?

But we must be honest and ask ourselves, Are we really living the normal Christian life as it is presented to us in the Scriptures? For it may be that our understanding of normal is no more than what we are now *used to*—all that happens to be within our current comfort zone. Our normal could be no more than what we have settled for, or what we have accepted as customary. Arthur Janov unpacks this concept further:

What usually happens [in any kind of testing for population norms] is that an average is calculated for the group, and that is called normal. But being average is not the same as being normal. . . . A normal blood pressure might be 110/70. Someone with a blood pressure of 180/110 is not normal. We know this empirically because consistently high blood pressure leads to disease such as stroke. But now we come to our first contradiction. Is the average blood pressure "normal"? It may be that the blood pressure of the general population from which we establish our norms is too high.[1]

And that's the same contradiction we must face in assuming what is normal for us, but in our case, the problem is reversed: Might our view of normal Christian living be much *too low?* By reframing the question about Christian living, we may be able to avoid that contradiction. Instead let's ask, What kind of Christian living is humanly *possible?* As those who have been created in the very image of God (Genesis 1:26), now regenerated and indwelt by God's Spirit, we must ask, What kind of human experience has God designed for us?

In part one, we addressed some of the challenges that may prevent us from growing in our God-confidence. For the remaining chapters of the book, we'll focus on what may contribute to expanding our God-confidence and our expectations of God's activity in this world. We begin part two by looking at what the Bible says about God-confidence. After a brief survey of God-confidence in the New Testament, we'll study key themes from Jesus' teachings. Then we'll take a closer look at Jesus' own lifestyle of trust in God, since he is our model for what a life of God-confidence can be. Remember that Jesus only taught us truths he had personally wrestled with and practiced in his own life. His teachings are never just "ivory tower" lectures or theories in the abstract. Whatever Jesus teaches comes from wisdom acquired by listening to and depending on God (John

8:28-29). He engaged in ministry based on the Father's view of reality. Jesus is the first person on earth to live his life in full reliance on God. Of course Jesus is God, even while he lived on this earth. But Jesus willingly limited direct access to his divine powers so he could experience humanity just as you and I experience it. He veiled his divine side so he could live a human life in dependence on God, showing us how to live a life of God-confidence in the power of the Holy Spirit.[2] These statements may raise some questions. The rest of the chapter will address these concerns to clarify what a life of biblical trust can look like.

Four New Testament Themes About God-Confidence

As a whole, the New Testament offers us four fundamental points about biblical God-confidence that will provide a general framework for our chapter. First, biblical God-confidence is belief *in* Jesus Christ (John 3:16; Acts 20:21; Colossians 1:4; 1 John 3:23). It is belief *in* God (Mark 11:22; Titus 3:8; Hebrews 6:1). There's a significant personal and relational dimension. As we grow in our relationship with God, we come to trust and rely on God more and more, just as in any human relationship. Asking what our relationship with God will be like in heaven, D. A. Carson suggests that even then we'll still have trust in God, because at its core God-confidence involves a *personal* relationship with God.

> Will we stop looking forward in anticipation to what is ahead once we begin to enjoy the new heaven and new earth? Consider faith: it is true that in one sense faith will be displaced by sight. But there is another sense in which faith is simply thankful trust in God, deep appreciation for him, committed subservience to him. Will there be any time in the next fifty billion years (if I may speak of eternity in the categories of time) during which the very basis of my presence in the celestial courts

will be something *other* than faith in the grace of God?[3]

Another aspect of biblical God-confidence requires that our minds and our worldviews be transformed by God to match Jesus' view of reality (Romans 12:1-2). Paul refers to these beliefs as "the faith" (e.g., Romans 1:5; Galatians 1:23; Ephesians 4:13; Colossians 2:7; 1 Timothy 2:7; 4:1). It includes having the correct knowledge and beliefs about God's reality. As long as we retain our existing naturalistic worldview of this present age, with its disregard of the supernatural, our journey in trusting in God will be stymied. We need a paradigm shift in our thinking. Chapters in part one focused on issues related to worldview and perceptions of reality.

Third, "faith without deeds is dead" (James 2:26). Our God-confidence will affect how we live (2 Corinthians 5:7; Galatians 2:20); it issues in action. We will need to step out and exercise our reliance by cooperating with God, relying on God's promises and trusting him for the results. Along with a paradigm shift, there also will need to be a practice shift. The chapters in part two will encourage taking more action steps of faith.

The fourth characteristic of God-confidence revealed in the New Testament is a pattern of progress and development of greater trust: our God-confidence can be strengthened (Colossians 2:7; 1 Thessalonians 3:2). It can grow more and more:

Our hope is that, as your faith continues to grow, our area of activity among you will greatly expand. (2 Corinthians 10:15)

We ought always to thank God for you, brothers [and sisters], and rightly so, because your faith is growing more and more, and the love every one of you has for each other is increasing. (2 Thessalonians 1:3)

As we mentioned earlier, our hope is that reading this book will help facilitate deepening your trust in a great and gracious God.

God is the supplier of our God-confidence, especially as it relates to spiritual gifts "in accordance with the measure of faith God has given you" (Romans 12:3; see also 1 Corinthians 12:9). And, as a part of that growth process, God will test us to examine and approve the quality of our trust in him (1 Peter 1:7; James 1:12), so that it yields greater Christlikeness (James 1:3).

Jesus' Amazing Teaching on Faith and Answered Prayer

Throughout his earthly ministry, Jesus encountered various reactions from people because of his teachings. Some were perplexed. Some were excited. Some were angry. Some were hopeful. But many times, people were simply shocked and amazed. One of the topics that sparked so much amazement among his followers was his collection of surprising promises about answered prayer. Consider this small sampling of Jesus' teachings on faith and prayer:

Ask and it will be given to you; seek and you will find; knock and the door will be opened to you. For everyone who asks receives; those who seek find; and to those who knock, the door will be opened.

Which of you, if your son asks for bread, will give him a stone? Or if he asks for a fish, will give him a snake? If you, then, though you are evil, know how to give good gifts to your children, how much more will your Father in heaven give good gifts to those who ask him! (Matthew 7:7-11 TNIV)

"Have faith in God," Jesus answered. "Truly I tell you, if you say to this mountain, 'Go, throw yourself into the sea,' and do not doubt in your heart but believe that what you say will happen, it will be done for you. Therefore I tell you, whatever you ask for in prayer, believe that you have received it, and it will be yours." (Mark 11:22-24 TNIV)

> Then Jesus told his disciples a parable to show them that they should always pray and not give up. . . . "And will not God bring about justice for his chosen ones, who cry out to him day and night? Will he keep putting them off? I tell you, he will see that they get justice, and quickly. However, when the Son of Man comes, will he find faith on the earth?" (Luke 18:1, 7-8)

> Very truly I tell you, all who have faith in me will do the works I have been doing, and they will do even greater things than these, because I am going to the Father. And I will do whatever you ask in my name, so that the Father may be glorified in the Son. You may ask me for anything in my name, and I will do it. (John 14:12-14 TNIV)

So what should we do with these incredible promises? How should we respond to Jesus' teaching, for example, from Matthew 17:20? "Because you have so little faith. I tell you the truth, if you have faith as small as a mustard seed, you can say to this mountain, 'Move from here to there,' and it will move. Nothing will be impossible for you." Truth be told, these promises about faith and prayer are as shocking for us today as they were for those in Jesus' time. The reality of every prayer answered as described in these verses doesn't match *our* experience. And we've not met anyone for whom it does. Since it doesn't resonate with our experience, we may be tempted to explain it away. But we must be cautious to avoid picking and choosing which of Jesus' teachings we'll rely on and which ones we won't simply because it *seems* far beyond what we could ever experience.

For example, Jesus also commanded us to "Be perfect, therefore, as your heavenly Father is perfect" (Matthew 5:48). Do we accept that Jesus only commands what is possible—though we may regard it as impossible? Perhaps keeping these two points in mind—to be developed later in the chapter—can help set the tone for the next two chapters: (1) Jesus' kingdom has come and *is now operational,* but (2) it will only be *fully and completely* operational in the next age. We know that when Jesus returns and when the new heavens and new earth are established, the old order will be over (Revelation 21:1-4). All will be set right and we ourselves will become perfect, for we will see God face to face (Revelation 22:5; compare Hebrews 12:14). Perfection is possible then, but not fully in this life. Yet Jesus urges us, by God's grace, to grow more and more into this kind of right living here and now: "Be perfect, therefore, as your heavenly Father is perfect" (Matthew 5:48).

As with most great moral teachers, Jesus is providing a vision, painting a picture of what a life fully lived in his kingdom looks like. Thus, we should read these statements as invitations to a journey of growth toward these ideals. They should not be read as impossible burdens Jesus is putting on our backs! Accordingly, the proper response is not: This is impossible. I could never get to this point. Rather it is: I hunger to enter more fully into this, and I will seek and learn toward that end. Thus, *each believer has the opportunity in the here and now to grow into a manner of living in which more answers to prayer are received than are currently occurring.* In the next two chapters we'll share the insights we've gained thus far regarding this biblical teaching.

God-Confidence and Plausibility Structures

A concept referred to in chapter one will provide some initial perspective on the matter. Within our views about the world and daily life, certain beliefs seem to us quite likely to be true (that professional football will not shut down in the near future), certain beliefs seem too incredible to rely on (that George Washington is just a myth; he never really existed), and certain beliefs run somewhere in between. An important part of our view of the world and daily life is our *plausibility structure.* It consists of a range of beliefs we have:

from those we hold with great certainty along a spectrum to those beliefs we hold with little certainty—but at least we might be willing to hear someone try to convince us about the matter.

For example, since it is not within our plausibility structure that the world is flat, people today would not even be willing to entertain this notion enough to attend a public lecture in its defense, much less actually trust it as true. On the other hand, it is in most people's plausibility structure today that near-death experiences (NDEs) are real glimpses of the other side. Because they find NDEs *plausible*, they listen with interest to television shows or read books that discuss this topic. Even among those who do not accept the reality of NDEs, such people would still regard them as plausible and would accordingly be willing to hear a case for them.

Outside of our plausibility structures are those ideas that we will *not entertain at all*. Perhaps we've never been confronted by them. Or perhaps we have and we've rejected them because they don't make any sense. But might there be some ideas outside of our plausibility structures that could in fact be true?[4]

Although certain aspects of Jesus' teaching on God-confidence and answered prayer may be part of those beliefs that lie outside of our plausibility structure, we can take comfort in knowing that our plausibility structures—our views of reality—can be altered. Let's look at two examples from Scripture where the disciples' plausibility structures were changed by their interactions with Jesus.

Resurrection day paradigm shift. Consider the case of the disciples after Jesus' death and the process it took for them to come to trust that Jesus had risen from the dead. On resurrection day, an angel announced to a group of women that Jesus was alive (Luke 24:4-10). They quickly returned and reported this to Jesus' disciples. But the disciples' response indicated that they did not consider the claim about Jesus being alive again as even possible; it was outside of their plausibility structures: "But they did not believe the women, because their words seemed to them like nonsense" (Luke 24:11). Peter and John ran to the site and were confronted by the evidence of the empty tomb. John began to grow in his trust for this truth based on seeing this evidence (John 20:8), though he admitted that he didn't yet fully understand what the Scriptures had foretold (John 20:9).

Later that day, Jesus suddenly appeared to the disciples (Luke 24:36-43), but Thomas was missing (John 20:24). "They were startled and frightened, thinking they saw a ghost. He said to them, 'Why are you troubled, and why do doubts rise in your minds? Look at my hands and my feet. It is I myself! Touch me and see; a ghost does not have flesh and bones, as you see I have'" (Luke 24:37-39). Then Luke records: "When [Jesus] had said this, he showed them his hands and feet. And while they still did not believe it because of joy and amazement, he asked them, 'Do you have anything here to eat?'" (Luke 24:40-41; Jesus invited them to act on this new belief by giving him food to eat, which also offered another proof he was alive in flesh and blood).

When the disciples reported to Thomas that they had seen Jesus, he replied, "Unless I see the nail marks in his hands and put my finger where the nails were, and put my hand into his side, *I will not believe it*" (John 20:25, emphasis added). The possibility of Jesus' resurrection was not within Thomas's plausibility structure. A week later Jesus finally appeared to Thomas and offered Thomas the opportunity to touch the nail marks and touch his side, saying: "Stop doubting and believe" (John 20:27). Thomas immediately blurted out, "My Lord and my God!" (John 20:28).

Scripture offers us a fascinating record of the worldview paradigm shift that took place in the disciples: from a place of distinct unbelief to a posture of belief in Jesus' resurrection after more evidence was available (e.g., empty tomb, Jesus eating food). In light of this case study, we may wish to ponder what ideas and concepts remain off the radar screen in our minds, outside the realm of our plausibility structure. Where are we currently being held hostage by closed minds, echoing Thomas's initial stance: *"I will not believe it"*? If we wish to move to a worldview like Jesus'—that this is a God-bathed world— we'll need to begin entertaining what we *consider* to be impossible.

Peter's experience of doubt and God-confidence. Consider another case from the Gospels that illustrates the same thing. Remember how the apostle Peter walked on water for a stretch, until the physical circumstances overwhelmed him (Matthew 14:24-33)? When Peter saw Jesus walking on the sea, he realized for the first time in his life that walking on the water was a real possibility. A belief component to biblical trust was awakened in Peter that matched the reality of God's kingdom, involving both material reality and immaterial reality. So, Peter immediately asked Jesus for permission to walk on the water, to come to Jesus. At the core of biblical trust is a growing personal relationship with God, not just relying on *our perception* of the reality God has created. In his request to Jesus, Peter also illustrates the third component of biblical trust: action. "'Lord, if it's you,' Peter replied, 'tell me to come to you on the water.' 'Come,' he said" (Matthew 14:28-29). Biblical trust requires actively living within and experiencing that new reality of this God-bathed world.

Peter got down out of the boat onto the water—literally took an action step of God-confidence—and walked toward Jesus. For a brief time, Peter expressed his reliance in God, and the water proved to be as solid as a hard floor. Imagine what Peter experienced. Do you think Peter just jumped out of the boat and ran toward Jesus? Or did he carefully lower himself out of the boat and gingerly test the water first, to see if one foot would stay on top of the water? When that first foot touched "solid water," Peter's God-confidence was strengthened to keep shifting his weight from the boat—from what he had known his whole life as a professional fisherman—to standing on the sea—to a brand new experience. Eventually he was away from the boat out on the sea walking toward Jesus. Peter saw the possibility and acted on that belief, trusting in Jesus' beckoning invitation that it was possible also for Peter to do what Jesus was doing.

But then his trust in God wavered and weakened. The waves distracted him. His concentration on Jesus and the new experience of walking on the water was interrupted. Fear crept in and overwhelmed his trust in Jesus. "But when [Peter] saw the wind, he was afraid and, beginning to sink, cried out, 'Lord, save me!' Immediately Jesus reached out his hand and caught him. 'You of little faith,' he said, 'why did you doubt?' And when they climbed into the boat, the wind died down" (Matthew 14:30-32). Imagine Jesus pulling Peter up back onto "solid water" and walking arm in arm on top of the water toward the boat. Jesus came along to strengthen Peter's God-confidence as they walked back to the boat. Only Peter was willing to take the risk; the others stayed "safe" in the boat.

There are critical moments in our journey in trusting God when we need to step out just like Peter into an inexperienced realm, taking God's Word and promises as the "real" representation of reality. Growing in biblical trust requires us to make a paradigm shift and a practice shift, *from* a primary confidence in this physical reality *to* a greater reliance in the immaterial reality of God's kingdom presently active in this world. We need to become much more sensitive to God's presence, becoming attuned to this invisible reality, where God is always near. Since God is not essentially material, God is immediately accessible to those who sincerely call upon him (Psalm 145:18; 2 Chronicles 16:9). Dallas Willard explains, "Every point in [the universe] is accessible to [God's] consciousness and will, and his manifest presence can be focused in any location as he sees fit. . . . So we should assume that space is anything but empty."[5]

In Psalm 139:7-12, King David declared that it is impossible to escape from God's presence. For many people living today, the only thing that exists is physical reality. We need not be limited by a physical world. Christians are invited to explore a whole new, immaterial realm of reality in God's kingdom. Furthermore, our understanding of who God is—the reality we hold to be true about God—affects how we'll live in this world. Yet no physical barrier or stretch of distance can ever prevent God from being present at any moment, within any situation, in our life. God is *always* near.[6] For "we live [primarily] by faith, not [only] by sight" (2 Corinthians 5:7). Though we may not all, like Peter, experience the exhilaration of walking on water, we all have the opportunity to trust God in unfamiliar circumstances.

Later we'll return to other concerns regarding Jesus' amazing promises and answered prayer, but let's consider other aspects of God-confidence that Jesus emphasized in his teaching.

Living by God-Confidence, Not by Sight

Jesus believed that, as Dallas Willard phrases it, "this is a God-bathed and God-permeated world."[7] The more we enter into Jesus' own view of reality, the more we can rely on that reality as he did. God-confidence is being able to see what those outside of God's family just cannot yet see. Central to Jesus' perspective was his view of God the Father. What does it mean when Paul says, "We live by faith, not by sight" (2 Corinthians 5:7)? Consider the verses that begin Paul's argument about the resurrection (2 Corinthians 4:16—5:10), which includes the directive to live by faith:

> Therefore we do not lose heart. Though outwardly we are wasting away, yet inwardly we are being renewed day by day. For our light and momentary troubles are achieving for us an eternal glory that far outweighs them all. So we fix our eyes not on what is seen, but on what is unseen. For what is seen is temporary, but what is unseen is eternal. (2 Corinthians 4:16-18)

The contrast is not just between physical reality and immaterial reality, although this can be one implication of the teaching as mentioned below. Primarily, Paul is highlighting that the present age, which includes suffering and pain, is fading away. And, the coming age of glory or God's kingdom project has already begun now, although it's not as perceptible to us as the present age. Paul Barnett clarifies: "Rather the dualism is eschatological, between this age and the coming age (see further [2 Corinthians] 5:1-5), and represents the reality that the believer lives in both simultaneously."[8] God is renewing us day by day, as a key part of his kingdom project that will fully come in the future. We need not get distracted by the seeming defeat or troubles of our daily lives ("what is seen"), because this affliction is actually being used by God to transform our character (2 Corinthians 3:18) so we can become the kind of citizens who will flourish in his future kingdom ("what is not seen").

Hebrews 11:1 makes a similar point: "Now faith is being sure of what we hope for and certain of what we do not see." George Guthrie explains, "Some realities are unseen because they belong to the [invisible and immaterial] spiritual realm and some because they lie in the future, when that realm will break into the earthly sphere. In either case, the person of faith lives out a bold confidence in God's greater realities."[9] God-confidence helps us look beyond the current troubling circumstances to rely on God's promises about the future. But trusting in God can also help us look beyond our present physical reality to rely on what is real though invisible and immaterial now.

Paul teaches us elsewhere that in our current condition we're not yet able to enter completely into the full and final version of God's kingdom—which unfolds when Jesus returns to earth at his second coming. Although Christians have already been saved and transferred into the kingdom of his Son (Colossians 1:13), we still live in this present age, having arenas of sin in our life, and physical bodies of this present age (Romans 8:23; 2 Corinthians 5:1). Paul tells us that "flesh and blood cannot inherit the kingdom of God, nor does the perishable inherit the imperishable" (1 Corinthians 15:50). We must be completely transformed, both in body and soul, for life in God's future kingdom.

Yet God is in the process of getting us ready for our future home (2 Peter 3:13). And the Holy Spirit who indwells all Christians is *the* sign or proof that all God's promises about the future will come to pass (God "has given us the Spirit as a deposit, guaranteeing what is to come," 2 Corinthians 5:5). Also, the Holy Spirit is the internal change agent for this transformation process (2 Corinthians 3:18). Second Corinthians 4:16 teaches that, while this present age continues on ("outwardly we are wasting away"), yet God has invaded this evil age in the person of Jesus Christ and is beginning his work among us now ("yet inwardly we are being renewed day by day"). That's the reality we can place our God-confidence in. Although God's kingdom is not *fully* here—we still await Christ's second coming—yet God's kingdom has already begun, inaugurated by Jesus himself, the King. Jesus' kingdom is genuinely operating now, but in a somewhat hidden and not fully realized manner within all Christians: "For you died, and your life is now hidden with Christ in God. When Christ, who is your life, appears, then you also will appear with him in glory" (Colossians 3:3-4). As George Ladd notes,

> Christ is now reigning as Lord and King, but his reign is veiled, unseen and unrecognized by the world. The glory that is now his is known only by [people] of faith. So far as the world is concerned, Christ's reign is only potential and unrealized. Nevertheless, contrary to appearances, he is reigning and "he must reign until he has put all his enemies under his feet" (I Cor. 15:25). Then his reign must become public in power and glory and his Lordship universally recognized (Phil. 2:10-11).[10]

These passages persuade us to place our reliance in God's kingdom project, that this "eternal" reality is now invading the "present," although it's not always possible to detect. The key to Christian living is: "we live by faith, not by sight" (2 Corinthians 5:7).

Peeking into the Heavens

Sometimes the supernatural breaks into the ordinary routines of life so obviously that we can't ignore what is usually a hidden realm. For example, on that momentous evening in Bethlehem two thousand years ago, a few shepherds on a late-night shift saw an angelic host burst on the scene with almost blinding brilliance, singing a joyful announcement of the birth of our Lord Jesus (Luke 2:8-14). In the book of Acts, Stephen, the first Christian martyr, saw a brief glimpse of heaven before he was stoned to death. God parted the heavens so that Stephen could gaze on unseen heavenly realities. "'Look,' he said, 'I see *heaven open* and the Son of Man standing at the right hand of God'" (Acts 7:56, emphasis added).

The prophet Elisha in the Old Testament was accustomed to this kind of heavenly visual. When the king of Syria kept trying to ambush the nation of Israel with his army, God always told Elisha the prophet about the Syrians' plans so Israel could avert being defeated by surprise. When the king found out that Elisha was the problem, he ordered his whole Syrian army to go and capture Elisha. Early the next morning when Elisha's servant went outside, he was horrified to see that the great Syrian army surrounded the city. But the servant didn't really see the full picture; in reality a far more powerful angelic host outnumbered the Syrian army. "'Don't be afraid,' the prophet answered. 'Those who are with us are more than those who are with them.' And Elisha prayed, 'O LORD, open his eyes so he may see.' Then the LORD opened the servant's eyes, and he looked and saw the hills full of horses and chariots of fire all around Elisha" (2 Kings 6:16-17). Later in Israel's history, the prophet Ezekiel was launched into his ministry with a view of normally unseen realities: "In the thirtieth year, in the fourth month on the fifth day, while I was among the exiles by the Kebar River, *the heavens were opened* and I saw visions of God" (Ezekiel 1:1, emphasis added).

There is more to reality than what we can see or touch. From these various reliable reports in Scripture, we can be assured that there is an unseen, invisible realm that is just as real as our physical realm. It's the realm in which God exists all the time. And it's even possible for some of us to get a *peek* into a realm that currently exists behind a "veil" (cf. Hebrews 6:19 NASB).

For example, God and angels exist though they are not material beings, as Mike Lambly came to realize. His little baby, week-old Katherine, was hanging on for dear life in an incubator at the neonatal unit of the hospital. That the one-pound, nine-ounce baby had lived that long was a miracle. Mike stopped by the hospital to check in on his little girl. While he was scrubbing up, he happened to look through the window at Katherine and was stunned at what he saw.

> Suddenly I stopped motionless over the basin, transfixed at the sight of two very large figures standing on either side of her incubator. They had to be at least ten feet tall, with very large shoulders. And they shone with the brightest white light I have ever seen. I could see no face to determine if the beings were male or female, but as I stared I knew they were angels and I was certain they were there to protect my daughter. The length of their appearance was very brief, and yet it seemed as if time stood still forever.[11]

Mike walked over to Katherine and assured her of Jesus' love as evidenced by the special angelic visitation. But the very next day Mike and his wife were informed that Katherine had passed away. A moving funeral service followed, but Mike still wondered why God had sent those angels. Two weeks later, Mike happened to watch a Billy Graham Crusade on television. Dr. Graham spoke on angels and mentioned that even in death God cares for his children. God sends his angels to take believers who have died to heaven. It dawned on Mike that the angels had come to take little Katherine into the very presence of God himself—what a comforting thought that was to him. There is much more to God's kingdom reality than we can imagine.

Living in the Tension in Between

But what about suffering? What about unanswered prayer? We do not have space to address these important issues—we have expressed our thoughts elsewhere[12]—but a few brief comments can be made. In this world, all believers are called to follow Jesus' example of suffering (1 Peter 2:21; Hebrews 5:7; John 15:17-18; e.g., Paul's suffering, 2 Corinthians 11:23-29; 2 Timothy 3:10-13). Believers experience various forms of suffering because of evil in the world (e.g., injustice, trauma, physical torture, martyrdom). As Paul encourages, we as a believing community need to "mourn with those who mourn" (Romans 12:15). We must come alongside to be the hands and feet of God, who comforts those in their pain (2 Corinthians 1:3-5). Do we as a Christian community offer designated times or meetings for public mourning, safe places to express lament to God? The largest category of Psalms is lament—journals of anguish, cries of despair for God's seeming absence (e.g., Psalms 22; 35).[13] In giving emphasis in this book to God's supernatural interventions in this world, we cannot ignore God's mysterious permission of horrendous evils and our calling as believers to suffer while standing against those evils.

On the other hand, Paul also exhorts us to "rejoice with those who rejoice" (Romans 12:15). Do we as a Christian community provide opportunities when the church gathers to share personal stories of how God intervened in miraculous ways? When there is something to rejoice about, we wish to share our joy with our friends—as in Jesus' parables of the lost sheep, lost coin and lost son (Luke 15:6, 9, 21-24, 32), where we learn there is much rejoicing in heaven when a person enters God's family (Luke 15:7, 10). It's not a matter of either-or, but of both/and: "Rejoice with those who rejoice; mourn with those who mourn" (Romans 15:12).

Furthermore, do we permit opportunity for the sick—for those who physically suffer—to be prayed for as commanded in James 5:14-15?

> Is anyone among you sick? Let them call the elders of the church to pray over them and anoint them with oil in the name of the Lord. And the prayer offered in faith will make them well; the Lord will raise them up. If they have sinned, they will be forgiven. (TNIV)

Douglas Moo notes that

> therefore, while not denying that some in the church may have the gift of healing, James encourages all Christians, and especially those charged with pastoral oversight, to be active in prayer for healing. . . . Similarly, James' promise that the Lord *will raise up (egeirō)* the sick person reflects the language of NT healing stories (Matt 9:6; Mark 1:31; Acts 3:7). Thus the picture is of the elders praying "over" the sick person in his bed and the Lord intervening to *raise him up* from that bed.[14]

We pray to God, and God raises some and does not raise others. It is God who heals, not our prayer alone. With confidence in God, we are obedient to his Word, so we mourn with those who mourn, we rejoice with those who rejoice, and we pray for those who are sick—and we leave the results up to God.

Several years ago, my (Klaus's) wife, Beth, experienced a "frozen" shoulder that would only move so far before the pain became excruciating. We regularly prayed for her and sought prayer from others. Yet God did not heal her supernaturally. She suffered through many months of pain. Eventually Beth had rotator-cuff surgery that was successful. We're thankful for medical technology as a means of alleviating physical pain. Soon after, her other shoulder froze up—a rare occurrence that both shoulders should have the same malady. We prayed for Beth, yet again God did not heal supernaturally. Following months of pain, the doctor performed the same surgery, successful as the previous one. Months after the first surgery, while at a weekend conference, Beth bowed her head in response to the speaker's suggestion that all attending pause and listen to what the Lord might say to each person. The Lord clearly spoke to Beth— recorded in her journal later that day—"Since your shoulder was injured, do you like how close we've become?" "Oh, yes!" Beth instantly responded, affirming the joy of this new level of intimacy. The Lord continued, "The pain will go on a little longer; and if I had healed you completely when you first asked, you would not have stayed open to me. Was the pain worth being able to have that [intimacy]?" "Oh, yes!" Beth immediately remarked, knowing in her heart the truth of these words, and comforted with the assurance of God's closeness and care, as she anticipated the beginning pains in her other shoulder.

I (Klaus) had an eye injury many years ago from playing Rollerblade hockey at my brother's cul-de-sac one fine Friday afternoon. At first I thought I might be blind in my left eye, but the main damage was a cataract. Yet the immediate danger was the profuse bleeding in my eye that could cause loss of sight. During the imposed stretch of three weeks lying in my bed to keep from moving my head in order to allow the bleeding to stop, I was challenged to pray persistently about my eye, to seek the Lord's healing. And the Lord surprised us with a "partial" healing. The eye doctor scheduled cleansing surgery for me within the next few days since my eye was not healing as it should. And we prayed each day for healing. On the morning of the surgery, before I was moved into the operating room, the doctor examined me closely one more time, and then suddenly canceled the operation! Enough cleansing had taken place since his previous examination a couple of days earlier to put me out of danger. He seemed to be shocked and asked, "What did you do?" Beth responded, "We prayed." Several months later, I underwent surgery for a lens implant to correct the traumatic cataract.

For the last couple of years, when I (J. P.) speak around the country I've asked audiences how many of them have ever experienced a miraculous healing that could not be explained any other way (for example, by placebo or coincidence). About 5 to 10 percent raise their hands. I then ask how many know someone who had such a miraculous healing and about 75 to 85 percent raise their hands. Of course, this is not a systematic survey and some overlap would occur with the 75 to 85 percent figure, yet knowing that God does intervene miraculously in the world can encourage our God-confidence that God may intervene in our circumstances and for those for whom we pray. R. T. France comments on Jesus' command to keep asking, keep seeking and keep knocking (Matthew 7:7-8):

> But for all that necessary caution [not everything we would like to have is granted], there is an openness about vv. 7-8 which invites not merely a resigned acceptance of what the Father gives, but a willingness to explore the extent of his generosity, secure in the knowledge that only what is "good" will be given, so that mistakes in prayer through human short-sightedness will not rebound on those praying.[15]

So we pray—exploring "the extent of his generosity"—and God works in ways we do not always understand (e.g., Job 1—2), sometimes through natural medical means, sometimes in miraculous ways and sometimes by being with us in the midst of our suffering. Could it be that we don't know more of God's generosity because we don't ask? ("You do not have, because you do not ask God," James 4:2[16]). Jesus' kingdom is here, yet not fully here, as D. A. Carson explains:

Already the kingdom has dawned and the Messiah is reigning, already the crucial victory has been won, already the final resurrection of the dead has begun in the resurrection of Jesus, already the Holy Spirit has been poured out on the church as the down payment of the promised inheritance and the first fruits of the eschatological harvest of blessings. Nevertheless, the kingdom has not yet come in its consummated fullness, death still exercises formidable powers, sin must be overcome, and opposing powers of darkness war against us with savage ferocity. The new heaven and the new earth have not yet put in an appearance. *Maintaining this balance is crucial to the church's maturity.*[17]

Jesus and the Disciples' Little Faith

Do you think it was unfair for Jesus Christ, second Person of the Godhead, to rebuke the disciples for their little faith (it appears Jesus coined a term, "little-faiths" [Greek, *oligopistoi*], e.g., Matthew 6:30; 8:26; 16:8)? What did Jesus really know about living by trust in God? After all, *he was God.* Wasn't it a bit unfair? Perhaps it's like someone today who inherited great wealth and lived their whole life without financial limits, trying to teach the rest of us how to live frugally on a budget. And then chiding us when we went over budget! Or like a musical prodigy, who played Beethoven's Fifth Symphony at six years old, expecting the rest of us with little musical training to play a complex concerto at first sight, and then rebuking us for making mistakes! How unfair!

How convinced are we that Jesus genuinely faced the challenges of life just like us? Was Jesus really human just like you and me? Was it the case that Jesus had access to something extra that is not readily accessible to all believers? Or, as we will consider in the pages that follow, if indeed Jesus needed to trust in God for his life and ministry—just as we do—then his teaching about God-confidence carries much more weight. So the question is, on the subject of having God-confidence, did Jesus actually practice what he preached? *Did Jesus need to trust in God?*

When Jesus came to earth, God himself took on human form, permitting a unique insider's view to experience what living humanly is really like. Philosophers use the term *de se* (pertaining to the self) to refer to firsthand knowledge of something. Sometimes it is best to do it oneself to demonstrate a point. For example, in 1921, Dr. Kane, the sixty-year-old chief surgeon of Kane Summit Hospital, successfully performed an appendectomy *on himself,* using only a local anesthetic, to demonstrate that ether was being used far too often when less dangerous local anesthetics could be used. In a similar manner, our God loves us so much that he became one of us, gaining firsthand experience of human living. Furthermore, one powerful benefit of Jesus' incarnation—of living on this planet for thirty-three years—is that we now have one who bears humanity within our trinitarian God, and one who prays for us (Romans 8:34), being able to identify with our experiences.

> For this reason [Jesus] had to be made like his brothers [and sisters] in every way, in order that he might become a merciful and faithful high priest in service to God. (Hebrews 2:17)

> For we do not have a high priest who is unable to sympathize with our weaknesses, but we have one who has been tempted in every way, just as we are—yet was without sin. (Hebrews 4:15)

Because Jesus took on human nature and experienced the joys of living and the suffering of this present age, Jesus became our sympathetic high priest, the unique mediator between God and humanity (1 Timothy 2:5) and our advocate (1 John 2:2) against the "accuser" (Revelation 12:10). As New Testament scholar, Luke Johnson, notes, "Jesus is not the mediator on the basis of his teachings or deeds, or even as an object of belief, *but on the basis of his very humanity:* Jesus is the representative human before the one God."[18]

Although here we are focusing on how Jesus is very much like us in his human experience, we also want to note that Jesus is unique and different from us; he is not *merely* human. For example, Scripture records Jesus' claims about himself being divine (e.g., Matthew 22:42-45; John 8:58-59) and his engagement in the activities of deity. For example, Jesus received worship (e.g., Matthew 28:9, 16; John 20:28), he made claims about his deity (e.g., Matthew 22:42-45; John 8:58-59), and the Gospel writers gave testimony to his deity (John 1:1, 18; use of the Old Testament word *Lord* for Jesus *[Yahweh]*, e.g., Luke 2:11; John 20:28). Jesus clearly teaches, "Anyone who has seen me has seen the Father" (John 14:9). But he is also human and so became the unique Anointed One/Messiah/Christ/Son of David (Luke 2:11; John 4:25-26). As the divine-human Savior, Jesus uniquely offered the substitutionary atonement for our sins (Mark 10:45; Romans 3:21-26).

So the question remains: Did Jesus express God-confidence himself? Not according to some theologians. For example, Thomas Aquinas thought that Jesus had the full beatific vision of God (Revelation 22:4) while a babe in the manger, thus requiring no need for any trust in God. Gerald O'Collins explains,

> Aquinas and the subsequent Catholic theological tradition held that in his human mind Jesus enjoyed the beatific vision and hence lived by sight, not by faith. Aquinas expressed classically this thesis: "When the divine reality is not hidden from sight, there is no point in faith. From the first moment of his conception Christ had the full vision of God in his essence. . . . Therefore he could not have had faith."[19]

Yet there is sufficient evidence in Scripture that Jesus was a person who relied on God himself. We'll look at three main lines of support: (1) passages discussing Jesus' God-confidence, (2) Jesus' claims of being dependent on God the Father (mainly from the Gospel of John) and (3) passages indicating Jesus' dependence on God the Holy Spirit (mainly from the Synoptic Gospels: Matthew, Mark and Luke).

Jesus' faith in Hebrews and in the Gospels. The view that Jesus did not need to express his own God-confidence perhaps influenced translators of Hebrews 12:2. They have inserted an *our* in the text where there is none in the Greek manuscripts: "looking to Jesus the pioneer and perfecter of *our* faith" (NRSV; so also, KJV, NIV and NET Bible). The NASB leaves the Greek as it is: "Fixing our eyes on Jesus, the author and perfecter of faith" (Hebrews 12:2). William Lane highlights the significance of this verse:

> The poignant description as a whole points to Jesus as the perfect embodiment of faith, who exercised faith heroically. By bringing faith to complete expression, he enabled others to follow his example. The phrase reiterates and makes explicit what was affirmed with a quotation from Scripture in [Hebrews] 2:13, that Jesus in his earthly life was the perfect exemplar of trust in God.[20]

Donald Hagner adds, "[Jesus] is not only the basis, means, and fulfillment of faith, but in his life he also exemplifies the same principle of faith that we saw in the paragons of [Hebrews] chapter 11."[21]

We might also point out that the New Testament writer to the Hebrews twice uses a distinctive word *archēgos* for Jesus (Hebrews 2:8; 12:2; cf. Acts 3:15). In various translations it appears as "pioneer" (NRSV) and "author" (NASB, NIV). It could also be translated as "initiator" or "forerunner." But in light of the athletic imagery, Lane proposes that we translate that word as "champion," which has some connection to the Greek tradition of Hercules. Thus Jesus is "the champion in the exercise of faith and the one who brought faith to complete expression."[22] Harold Attridge agrees and offers additional insight for *archēgos*.

> Of equal importance is the fact that [Jesus] provides a perfectly adequate model of what life under that covenant involves. Thus the "faith" *[pisteōs]* that Christ inaugurates and brings to perfect expression is not the content of Christian belief, but the fidelity and trust that he himself exhibited in a fully adequate way and that his followers are called upon to share. . . . It is precisely as the one who perfectly embodies faith that he serves as the ground of its possibility in others [*archēgos-aitios* ("source")] and the model they are to follow [*archēgos-prodromos* ("forerunner," Heb 6:20)].[23]

In the Gospels, note the father's honest response to Jesus about his lack of trust in God. The exchange went like this:

> Jesus asked the boy's father, "How long has he been like this?"
> "From childhood," he answered. "It has often thrown him into fire or water to kill him. But if you can do anything, take pity on us and help us."
> "'If you can'?" said Jesus. "Everything is possible *for him who believes.*"
> Immediately the boy's father exclaimed, "I do believe; help me overcome my unbelief!" (Mark 9:21-24)

Jesus' response in Mark 9:23 (in italic) is a challenge to the father, but also a testimony of his own life of God-confidence. Sharyn Dowd explains, "Jesus is not merely an example to be imitated, but a leader to be followed. It is likely, then, that 'the one who believes' in [Mark] 9:23 is deliberately ambiguous. Jesus has faith and he calls the father to have faith."[24] O'Collins agrees: "[Jesus] speaks about faith as an insider, one who knows personally what the life of faith is and wants to share it with others."[25] If Jesus was a man of reliance on God himself, then when he criticizes the disciples for their lack of trust (e.g., Matthew 6:30; 8:26; 16:8; *oligopistoi* [little faiths]), he speaks as one who experientially knows what he is talking about. Ian Wallis notes, "The disciples may have been ineffectual . . . owing to their *oligopistia* [little faith], but Jesus was successful because he demonstrated that faith . . . a faith which all who intend to fulfill Christ's commission must demonstrate."[26]

Jesus' dependence on God the Father. Next, Jesus often talked about his complete dependence on the Father. Here are a few Scriptures (with pertinent clauses italicized) that attest to this fact:

> I tell you the truth, *the Son can do nothing by himself;* he can do only what he sees his Father doing, because whatever the Father does the Son also does. (John 5:19)

> So Jesus said, "When you have lifted up the Son of Man, then you will know that I am the one I claim to be and that *I do nothing on my own but speak just what the Father has taught me.* The one who sent me is with me; he has not left me alone, for I always do what pleases him." (John 8:28-29)

> For I did not speak of my own accord, but the Father who sent me commanded me what to say and how to say it. I know that his command leads to eternal life. So whatever I say is just *what the Father has told me to say.*" (John 12:49-50)

Similar declarations appear also in John 5:30; 7:28-29; 8:42; 14:10, 31; 15:9-10, 15; 16:32; and 17:8, 18.

In John 15:5, Jesus draws a parallel between his own relationship with the Father (John 5:19, quoted above) and our relationship to Jesus: "I am the vine; you are the branches. If a man remains in me and I in him, he will bear much fruit; apart from me *you can do nothing*" (emphasis added). Jesus offers himself as an example of dependency for believers. The Epistles reinforce this teaching (e.g., Colossians

3:15-17). Even our prayer requests, although directed to the Father, should be "in the name of Jesus" (e.g., John 15:7, 16; 16:23; John 14:14; see also Matthew 6:9; Ephesians 3:14).

Jesus depended on God the Holy Spirit. The New Testament teaches that Jesus himself expressed God-confidence, with statements about his faith/trust, as well as statements about Jesus' dependence on the Father. But another indication of Jesus' God-confidence is his reliance on the Holy Spirit.

The New Testament closely associates Jesus with the ministry of the Spirit (passages are listed in chronological order, emphasis added):

> Jesus, full of *the Holy Spirit,* returned from the Jordan and was led by *the Spirit* in the desert, where for forty days he was tempted by the devil. . . . [Following the temptation] Jesus returned to Galilee in the power of *the Spirit.* (Luke 4:1-2, 14)

> [Jesus, reading from Isaiah 61:1,] "'*The Spirit* of the Lord is on me.' . . . Today this scripture is fulfilled in your hearing." (Luke 4:18, 21; see also John 3:34; Isaiah 11:2)

> But if I drive out demons by the *Spirit of God,* then the kingdom of God has come upon you. (Matthew 12:28)

> You know what has happened throughout Judea . . . how God anointed Jesus of Nazareth with *the Holy Spirit* and power, and how he went around doing good and healing all who were under the power of the devil, because God was with him. (Acts 10:37-38; see also Acts 1:2)

To explore this idea a bit further, let's look at two Gospel episodes: Jesus' casting out of a demon (Matthew 12:28, 32) and his agony in the Garden of Gethsemane (Matthew 26:41 = Mark 14:38). "But if I drive out demons by the Spirit of God, then the kingdom of God has come upon you" (Matthew 12:28; "by the finger of God," Luke 11:20[27]). Beasley-Murray notes that "it gives Jesus' own explanation of his exorcisms: they are performed not by his own power but by the power of God, i.e., by the Spirit of God, and since the defeat of the evil power is a feature of the end time, they show that the kingdom of God has appeared in his activity."[28] Furthermore, Jesus makes a follow-up comment about the blasphemy of the Holy Spirit (Matthew 12:32), which illustrates how deeply Jesus felt about the relation he sustained to the Holy Spirit: "it scatters to the winds the idea that he attached little importance to the Holy Spirit in his ministry."[29]

During Jesus' struggle in prayer in the Garden of Gethsemane, he had asked his disciples to pray for him, yet he found them asleep. In his response, he says, "Watch and pray so that you will not fall into temptation. The spirit is willing, but the body is weak" (Matthew 26:41; Mark 14:38). A common view is that Jesus was concerned about a continuing internal struggle within human nature, between the human spirit and the weak physical body. According to this view, Jesus' comment is a challenge to muster more human effort to overcome bodily weakness in order to pray and avoid temptation. But consider another interpretation. In this case the contrast is between relying on divine power of the Holy Spirit and relying solely on human resources (flesh), for the humanity on its own can never stand against the assaults of Satan. To confirm this view, Jesus made similar contrasts elsewhere between the divine sphere and the human sphere (John 3:6; 6:63), which have Old Testament precedent. In Isaiah 31:1, 3, a contrast is made between relying on Egypt's military might (flesh) and relying on the Lord God (spirit; see also Psalm 51:11-12). William Lane comments on Mark 14:38,

> Spiritual wakefulness and prayer in full dependence upon divine help provide the only adequate preparation for crisis. . . . Jesus prepared for his own intense trial through vigilance and prayer, and thus gave to the disciples and to the Church the

model for the proper resistance of eschatological temptation.[30]

Here Jesus offers his disciples the secret to his own victory in the garden, thus furnishing the most explicit reference to his own dependence on the Holy Spirit and a teaching for all believers for all times. *Depend on Holy Spirit.*

Furthermore, a common misperception is that Jesus' relationship with the Spirit only began at his baptism, when Jesus was specially anointed for his messianic ministry. Quite the contrary, the Holy Spirit had been a constant companion of Jesus since his conception. Note Gabriel's message to Mary: "The Holy Spirit will come upon you, and the power of the Most High will overshadow you. So the holy one to be born will be called the Son of God" (Luke 1:35). In addition, Luke offers implicit references to the Spirit, in contrast to the explicit note regarding John the Baptist's childhood. Note the parallels. "And the child [John the Baptist] grew and became strong in spirit" (Luke 1:80). "And the child [Jesus] grew and became strong; he was filled with wisdom, and the grace of God was upon him" (Luke 2:40). If Messiah's forerunner was filled with the Spirit from birth (Luke 1:15), surely also the Messiah himself was filled with the Spirit from birth—to whom the Father gave the Spirit without measure (John 3:34-35).

Note what Scripture teaches about the twelve-year-old Jesus. He astounded the teachers with "his understanding and his answers" (Luke 2:47). Earle Ellis notes that Luke 2:47 is not intended

> just as a tribute to Jesus' intelligence but as a witness to his relationship to God. . . . The same "Holy Spirit" power, later to be manifested in Jesus' ministry, even now is at work. Jesus interprets the Scripture not from the knowledge gained in rabbinic training but from the "wisdom" given by God.[31]

Luke closes this episode with this summary statement, "Jesus grew in wisdom and stature, and in favor with God and men" (Luke 2:52).[32] Jesus and the Holy Spirit experienced a continuing and intimate relationship from the very beginning of Jesus' life.[33]

The biblical teaching is clear that, while on this earth, Jesus walked in dependence upon God the Father and in the Holy Spirit—Jesus himself experienced trust in God to live his life and carry out his ministry. Thus when Jesus speaks about the topic of faith, he knows of what he speaks. Jesus' example of faith encourages and challenges us to deepen our God-confidence.

Making Sense of Jesus' Promises

So the question remains: What do we make of Jesus' teaching about God-confidence and answered prayer? Should we dismiss it and claim that Jesus doesn't understand what is *real* in the contemporary world? Or should we admit that, although this truth is within Jesus' plausibility structures, it may not be within ours. Should we submit to our Abba and confess, "I do believe; help me overcome my unbelief!" (Mark 9:24)? Is our curiosity sufficiently piqued to ponder the matter further, to seek further information, just as the two disciples ran to see the empty tomb for themselves?

Truthfully, if we want to let biblical truth lead the way in our worldview formation, then we must not allow our own limited experiences to hinder our journey into greater reliance in God. As evangelicals, we want to trust what the Bible teaches, and not depend on what our own limited experiences confirm about reality—that's like relying on an argument from silence.[34] Jesus teaches that much more is possible. To acquire the amazing worldview Jesus had, we'll need to be willing to let go of our small and limited views of God and his world. As we become more receptive to God's amazing truth, it will illumine the way out of darkness and doubt to a reality and power that is very real—so real that even Peter could walk on water as Jesus bid him come.

But can we truly have God-confidence like Jesus? Is that possible?

"I do believe; help me overcome my unbelief!" (Mark 9:24). This frantic response to Jesus from the concerned father can become an important confession of our own hearts as we desire to live a life of God-confidence. Each believer operates from a degree of reliance on God. And yet, we still have areas of limited trust in God, areas in which our God-confidence needs to deepen. Like Peter on the water, into what new realm is Jesus inviting us?

One thing Jesus wanted for his disciples was that they exercise greater God-confidence (e.g., Matthew 17:19-20). Eventually, as recorded in the book of Acts, these disciples exercised more of the kind of trust Jesus had. For example, they boldly proclaimed the good news about Jesus in the face of severe opposition (Acts 5:18-42; 16:16-40). We want to highlight in this chapter that it's possible even to exercise our *little* God-confidence and see God work. And it's also possible for our reliance on God to increase. Furthermore, it's a process God nurtures in us as we step out in obedience. It's an invitation God offers his beloved children, to experience much more of his kingdom realities this side of heaven. As we'll see, a key goal in Jesus' school of discipleship is that we step out and exercise our God-confidence, and we'll find that our reliance in God will grow as a result.

Stepping Out in Trust

Jesus teaches us that there is much more to life than what meets the eye. Living by God-confidence involves becoming more aware of this reality and becoming convinced it's real and reliable—and then stepping out with trust, as Peter stepped over the gunwale of the boat and started walking on the sea. There needs to be a *worldview paradigm shift,* a change in our understanding of reality—to match what really is the case. False beliefs need to be identified and give way to true beliefs by a process of being exposed to reality. I (Klaus) remember that as a young child I had the belief that on Sunday it would never rain, that the sun would always shine because it was SUN-day! Imagine my shock the first day I noticed that it rained on Sunday! Reality crashed in on my naive assumptions about the world. Actually, it was a bit of a crisis of God-confidence. My view of reality needed reshaping, and I had to realize that I had no basis for blaming God for my wrong belief. As explained in chapter one, our beliefs are changed indirectly. Growing in knowledge is one key component for nurturing our God-confidence.

Becoming a member of God's family requires a series of paradigm shifts for each of us regarding our worldview. For example, beliefs have to be confirmed that God exists, that Jesus actually is our Savior, and that we can relinquish our life (for me, "life" was the extent I knew then as an eleven-year-old) and place our life in his trust. A more recent example of a major paradigm shift for me was the new belief that God would speak to me personally. For most of my life this idea was not within my plausibility structures. I had learned within my tradition that, since the Bible was completed, we didn't need any personal word from God. The Bible was the complete special revelation of God, sufficient for salvation and our Christian life. And I've dedicated my life to studying the Bible. But it never occurred to me that God also can give me personal guidance—as if I could limit whatever God could do. [35]

The idea was introduced to me by a credible witness, someone I trusted, who knew God and the Bible well. I started exploring the matter over a period of time and moved from skepticism to belief. I'm convinced that the Bible actually teaches this. For example, when King David had to flee quickly from Jerusalem during his son Absalom's rebellion, the king encountered a man throwing sticks and mud at him. With shrill curses, Shimei shouted at the king, "Get out, get out, you man of blood, you scoundrel!" (2 Samuel 16:7). Imagine what the king could have done! His general wanted to lop off Shimei's head for such disrespect. But David viewed the matter differently. He considered the possibility that God could be speaking to him through this bizarre episode. "If he is cursing because the LORD said to him, 'Curse David,' who can ask, 'Why do you do this?'" (2 Samuel 16:10; note Psalm 32:8-9, penned by David).

Once I became convinced that God often gives personal guidance to his children, I remembered a particular time I was speechless at a professional conference where I was presenting a workshop. During the question-and-answer time, my mind went blank. I had nothing to say. Then suddenly I had the answer, and it was a good one. At the time I thought I was a genius, but now I realize God the Holy Spirit had bailed me out. In the final chapter, we'll return to this important topic of God's personal guidance as one instance for stepping out with trust.

Practice Shift: Practical Ways to Grow in God-Confidence

However, if only a paradigm shift takes place and there is no change in lifestyle, the process has been aborted. James tells us that "faith without deeds is dead" (James 2:26); if there is no life-related change, then there is no functional God-confidence. There also needs to be a *practice shift*. In some cases, the practice shift takes place first, then can follow the paradigm shift in belief. For example, someone may offer a desperate prayer to God for help, even though that person doesn't think God exists. Our pastor Lance Pittluck offered such a prayer as a young seeker: "Show me if you're real. If you're not, you won't hear this prayer anyway." God showed up. Lance was in a Bible study exploring the Gospel of John. But up to that point, it made no sense to him. "It might as well have been written in Chinese," he says. After that prayer, God opened Lance's spiritual eyes and it all began to make sense. As a result, Lance moved toward a posture of greater reliance on God's existence. Charles Kraft, veteran missionary and cultural anthropologist, reminds us that both kinds of shift need to take place: "The real key, though, is that changes in both *belief* and *practice* are necessary if true worldview change is to take place."[36]

Thus, we must exercise our God-confidence if we want our trust in God to have its full effect in our lives and in the lives of others. To grow in God-confidence, we must step out of the comfort zones of the routines of life and begin relying on a reality that is now unseen to us. Since both of us come from the academic arena, we have reflected on the small step of God-confidence that Dr. Michael Atchison took in his classroom at the University of Pennsylvania that has had profound results. Since 1989 he's been a professor in the biochemistry department of animal biology. Dr. Atchison would clearly identify himself as a Christian in his science classes at the university, but he often wondered whether being a classroom biochemistry teacher ever made any difference for God's kingdom.

> It was a little hard to be certain that this was really a high impact ministry. It was gratifying that some students were appreciative of my statements, but it was unclear how useful were my efforts. I know that with faith as small as a "mustard seed," I should be able to move mountains. But I didn't really see how this was moving mountains. That was, until the Lord gave me a peek at His power to move mountains.[37]

In a class he taught, one of his students was the wife of an editor at Free Press, a major New York publisher. The editor (her husband) had received a manuscript written by a biochemist on the subject of intelligent design that was a critique of Darwinian evolution. The editor was concerned whether anyone beyond the academic community would want to read the book. His wife encouraged him to call her professor. One day Dr. Atchison received a phone call from this Free Press editor, without knowing how the contact was made. During the ten-minute conversation, Dr. Atchison affirmed the need for a book like this, that origin-of-life issues were still important matters beyond academia. The book was published two years later: *Darwin's Black Box* (New York: Free Press, 1996) by Michael J. Behe. It became an instant bestseller, being named *Christianity Today*'s Book of the Year in 1996. Dr. Behe is now a key leader in the intelligent design movement. Dr. Atchison notes that by identifying himself as a Christian in his classroom, he "played a small, but crucial part in influencing" all those who have benefited from the publication of that book.

Stepping out with trust in God will require our action and will probably involve some kind of stretch on our part. It will require some risk. One implication from Jesus' parable of the talents is that the Christian life involves risk (Matthew 25:14-30). How else could the two servants engage in business and double the money entrusted to them? Wise risks are part and parcel of the life of God-confidence. The writer to the Hebrews says it this way: "And without faith it is impossible to please God, because anyone who comes to him must believe that he exists and that he rewards those who earnestly seek him" (Hebrews 11:6). God rewards our steps of trusting to seek him and his kingdom (Matthew 6:33).

In the final chapter of this book, we'll focus on one form of God-confidence-stretching activity: in regard to finding God's direction and personal guidance, we'll explore the various ways—some old and some new—that God can use to communicate his personal thoughts to us. We'll close this chapter by briefly suggesting a few God-confidence-nurturing projects related to the four New Testament themes about God-confidence identified at the beginning of the chapter (see table 4.1). Below, we'll provide a little more detail on the first two projects listed in the table; the final two are self-explanatory.

1. The personal/relationship dimension of biblical trust. Connecting with God and conversing with God more regularly throughout our day can help us grow relationally closer to God. One way to do

Table 4.1. God-Confidence-Nurturing Projects

1. *Personal/relational* (Mark 11:22; Ephesians 3:12): trusting in God	Press the "pause button" of life to connect regularly with God through your day.
2. *Content/worldview* (Ephesians 4:13): "the faith," what we hold to be true about reality	a. Read, study and meditate on the Gospels. b. Find "credible witnesses" and learn from them (e.g., read this chapter and continue to bring before your mind one key concept).
3. *Action* (James 2:26): trust expressed in action	Experiment and step out in God-confidence, relying on a promise of God. Make a "faith-stretching" request of God.
4. *Progression* (2 Corinthians 10:15): growth of God-confidence	Keep a journal of your God-confidence projects: What are you doing and why? Now and then, reread your journal to see what changes are taking place in your God-confidence.

that is by pressing the pause button of life, to keep in contact with the God who is always near. The analogy comes from a video or DVD player. If the phone rings while we're watching a movie, we press the pause button to put the movie on hold and answer the phone. Then we just press the pause button again to return to the movie. Why not take several brief pause breaks with God during your day? Put life on hold for thirty seconds and turn your attention God-ward. Perhaps you can place some visual cues around your life to help remind you to press the pause button—little stickies on the bathroom mirror, computer screen, car dashboard. As these pause breaks become a habit throughout your day, they can help you increase your awareness that God exists not only on Sunday but every day of the week, and every moment of every day. And with these regular pause breaks you'll be more aware of God's nearness—something Jesus had confidence in at the depth of his soul.

2. Worldview formation. In the first chapter we noted that formation of worldview beliefs takes place indirectly over time. The key is to read, study and meditate on matters we wish to grow into. One thing we've found beneficial is to identify a few "credible witnesses," Christian leaders whom you can trust, who have a growing and dynamic relationship with God, who evidence a life of biblical trust themselves. Read their writings and biographies to be challenged to live more and more within God's kingdom reality. Find out where they're speaking and attend these conferences. Learn about the new arenas God's taking them in their God-confidence walk, for we all can keep growing in our reliance on God. Our hope is that our book will become a helpful resource, that we've become credible witnesses to enable you to explore the matter of biblical trust further. Perhaps read this chapter again. What one concept is God challenging you to develop in your God-confidence? You may wish to read some of the books we've listed in our footnotes. We have also greatly benefited from reading and studying the Gospels, for Jesus is the best credible witness, one who demonstrates fully what a life of God-confidence looks like.

One picture of what exercising God-confidence can look like is the image of Peter lifting his leg out of the boat and gingerly stepping out on the "solid" water. Or we could imagine learning to ice skate for the first time. It's a bit uncomfortable at first—we slip and fall a lot. But with persistence and practice we can become adept ice skaters. Gradually we learn to function well in a new-to-us environment. And so it will be as our God-confidence increases. If we wish to grow in our reliance on God, we'll need to follow Jesus' advice: keep seeking, keep asking, keep knocking (Matthew 7:7-11). C. S. Lewis said it well, "Aim at heaven and you get earth thrown in. Aim at earth and you will get neither."[38]

In this chapter we've shared mostly biblical accounts of what it might look like to rely on Jesus' incredible promises. But are there contemporary reports that illustrate this kind of supernatural living? In the next chapter we provide a number of amazing case studies, demonstrations of God's continuing intervention in the lives of believers today. We hope that reading the next chapter will bolster your confidence in Jesus' teaching about faith with the result that your God-confidence will increase.

True faith is never found alone; it is always accompanied by expectations. The [person] who believes the promises of God expects to see them fulfilled. Where there is no expectation there is no faith.

A. W. TOZER, *GOD TELLS THE MAN WHO CARES*

Questions for Personal Application and Group Discussion

1. How would you describe the normal Christian life? Where does your understanding of the normal Christian life come from? How is your view reflected in your daily life?

2. In your own words, describe the four fundamental themes that the New Testament teaches about God-confidence—see pages 97-98 and table 4.1 on page 130. Why is each of these aspects important to the way we understand what the Bible teaches about God-confidence? Which of the projects in table 4.1 would you like to try out this week?

3. Take a moment to review and reflect on the Scripture verses listed on pages 99-100 that contain Jesus' promises regarding faith and answered prayer. In your journal or small group, discuss your response to these promises.

4. Do you agree or disagree with the authors' claim that any change in our beliefs must ultimately result in a change in our practice? Why or why not?

5

BEARING WITNESS TO
GOD'S ACTIVITY IN OUR WORLD

If you had to guess, what would you identify as the most prominent source of doubt in America today? Is it certain discoveries of science? Incredulity about some stories in the Bible? The intolerance of Jesus' claims to be the only way? These are not even close. In his study of doubt and defection from Christianity, sociologist Christian Smith claims that far and away the chief source of doubt comes from God's apparent inactivity, indifference or impotence in the face of tragedy and suffering in the respondents' lives and in others' lives, and the apparent lack of God's interventions and help in the toil and fatigue of daily troubles.[1]

Just the other day, J. P.'s wife, Hope, made her weekly visit to a shelter for women with various addictions. As she was teaching the Scriptures and ministering to the women, a new resident at the shelter interrupted her by announcing that she was an atheist. When asked why she held to this view, without hesitation she bemoaned that she had often called out to God, as had others she knew, and no one answered. Since (allegedly) no one answered, she concluded that no one was on the other end of the line.

In light of his study, Smith claims that spiritual experiences are a major source of development in trust in God and strengthening of that trust: "Very many modern people have encountered and do encounter what are to them very real spiritual experiences, frequently vivid and powerful ones. And these often serve as epistemological anchors sustaining their religious faith in even the most pluralistic and secular of situations."[2]

With two qualifications, we believe Smith is onto something very important. First, spiritual experiences in themselves can be dangerous and misleading, so they cannot sustain on their own the weight of religious, especially Christian, conviction. However, given a framework of objective biblical revelation (e.g., Jesus' promises developed in the last chapter) and a biblically pregnant view of God-confidence that includes the various factors covered in this book, experiences of the triune God, his love and mercy, and his responses to prayer are powerful sources of encouragement and confirmation of reliance on God. Second, since Christian growth is a communal and not merely an individualistic endeavor, we would expand Smith's frame of reference from personal experiences of God to include hearing of, even experiencing, his presence and actions vicariously in and through the lives of others.

Let's Go Witnessing

As evangelicals, we know that regular, thoughtful, open-hearted exposure to God's Word strengthens God-confidence. But what we often miss out on is regular exposure to the art of testimony—witnessing—to the great acts of God on behalf of his corporate people or individuals.

One of the essential, regular practices of the Old Testament people of God was to overcome fear, weakness of heart, cowardice and failing trust in God by recalling the actions of God in the distant or recent past. For example, when the Israelites faced intimidation and mockery from their enemies, Nehemiah reenergized and strengthened their God-confidence by bearing witness to the great deeds of

God on Israel's behalf (Nehemiah 9). In the Old Testament, this sort of recollection and testifying was directed at God's actions on behalf of the worshiping community (Psalm 44) or an individual believer (Psalm 18).

When we turn to the New Testament, we see the same thing: witness is borne to the deeds of Jesus and his Spirit to bring about or increase God-confidence (e.g., in John 19:35; 21:24-25; Acts 10:39). In fact, the major reason why the Bible contains so much historical narrative instead of coming to us as a systematic theology text in which doctrine after doctrine is clarified and affirmed is because a central affirmation of Christianity is that God is a *living* God. As such, he is a God who acts, manifests himself and communicates in many ways with his children.

In our experience, a main source of increasing God-confidence is *hearing and bearing witness* to answers to prayer, to the Lord guiding and speaking in various ways, to miracles of healing, and to deliverance from spiritual warfare and demonization.

Skepticism Regarding the Supernatural

Unfortunately, many believers are suspicious, even skeptical, of the supernatural. In fact, many would refrain from labeling something as a supernatural manifestation of God, an angel or a demon even if they saw it with their own eyes. As a result, when believers see a miracle, they are afraid of sharing it because they don't want to appear weird or gullible to others.

Not long ago I (J. P.) was invited to address the staff of a large church in Southern California on the topic of nurturing the God-confidence of their church. Among other things, I noted that reliance on God grows as people share with one another how God had intervened in their lives. I also urged them to find ways to encourage such sharing. As we were taking a coffee break, a young man on the church staff approached me rather sheepishly and began to share something from his own journey. As he shared, it became obvious that this was something he usually kept to himself. Four years earlier, he told me, he was in a machine shop when heavy machinery fell on him and fractured his chest and hands. He was rushed to the doctor, x-rayed and sent home that evening with pain medication. He was scheduled to come back the next morning for further examination and treatment.

That evening, some Christian friends came to his house and prayed for his healing. Even though he was on pain medication, he could still feel pain; however, as the people prayed, the pain vanished and the swelling in his hands left. He was startled. The next morning, the surgeons took new x-rays, which indicated that the fractures were completely healed. The doctors also noted that the swelling was gone, something that just does not happen so quickly on its own. When the doctors compared the two sets of x-rays, it was clear that he had been miraculously healed! The fracture lines were gone!

Needless to say, I was deeply moved by his story. But I was shocked when I asked him if he had ever shared this story with anyone. He responded that he had kept the story to himself because he didn't want to talk about himself or appear weird to people. It seems to us that he had missed a golden opportunity to strengthen the God-confidence of others by bearing witness to God's acts on his behalf. In order to encourage each other that the Christian life is a supernatural journey, we must be willing to share these sorts of things with others. We need to provide opportunities for credible testimonials to be given to each other on a regular basis because they strengthen people's confidence in God and his Word.

While we, as well as many others, find this young man's story to be very encouraging, his concern about appearing weird is valid, for some may remain a bit skeptical and hesitant about stories like this. There are many reasons for this skepticism, but a major factor is the influence on believers of the pervasive *naturalism* in our culture. As a result, says Chuck Kraft,

> In the present day, Evangelicals tend to believe that God has stopped talking and doing the incredible things we read about in scripture. Now we see God limiting himself to working through the Bible . . . , plus an occasional contemporary "interference" in the natural course of events. What we usually call a miracle—the power God used to manifest in healing—has been largely replaced by medicine. The speaking he used to do now comes indirectly through rationalistic reasoning in books, lectures, and sermons—similar to the process used by secular scientists.[3]

In many ways, this entire book is an attempt to offset the influence of naturalism on the development of God-confidence among believers, but Kraft identifies three additional inhibiting factors to deepening our faith.[4]

1. We have a fear of risking and looking foolish if we pray for the sick and nothing happens. A major purpose for hearing and giving testimony to God's acts on our behalf is that such testimony builds God-confidence so that people are more eager to step out and trust God in new ways. And this always involves some sort of risk. But regardless of the potential risks, the question remains: Would you rather play it safe and never see much happen in the spiritual realm? Or would you rather step out, take some faith-risks, fail from time to time, see God not show up as you had hoped, but also have the opportunity of seeing genuine confidence-inducing answers to prayer and other miracles?

In our own personal lives and ministries, we have opted for the latter alternative. We would rather pray for two hundred sick people and see five be healed than pray for ten and see nothing happen. For two years we have devoted more time to praying for the sick than ever before in our Christian lives. Months ago, we were speaking at a conference in which a young lady who had a damaged knee received healing prayer. She had been on crutches for about a month and walked with a serious limp, and she had not exercised for two full months. After receiving prayer, she was completely healed. She began walking normally (and does so to this very day) and returned the next morning to her daily routine of jogging, all with no pain at all!

2. We have a stereotype that people involved in these things are weird, uneducated and, in extreme cases, frauds. We empathize with this concern, but if one is not careful, adherence to it can throw the proverbial baby out with the bathwater. The result will be a missed opportunity to strengthen one's God-confidence. Consider these two points. First, God sometimes asks his children to do some pretty weird things: Joshua and his band to walk around Jericho, Isaiah to go naked for three years, Hosea to marry a practicing prostitute. We must be very careful in labeling something weird. Of course, weirdness for weirdness' sake is wrong. And while we must always approach things with wisdom and discernment, this admission must not become an excuse to become a naysayer. Instead, we should adopt a spirit of wise, gracious, seeking hunger for God and his glory.

Second, we admit that there is truth to the stereotype, and, indeed, some of the things done in the name of the Spirit are fraudulent. But one does not determine the proper use of the real thing (e.g., how to use real money) by focusing on the abuse of a counterfeit. Proper caution is not the same thing as unbelief.

3. Christians who hold to a doctrine of cessationism also tend to avoid expecting that God can still work miracles today. Cessationism is an interpretation that the miraculous gifts (e.g., healings, prophecy, words of knowledge and wisdom, demonic discernment, miracles, tongues and their interpretation) have ceased and that their exercise is not for today. There are two ways to respond to this issue. First, whether these particular gifts are still operating today is really a secondary issue. Dan Wallace, a New Testament scholar who holds to cessationism, has recently edited a book to challenge cessationists to pray more for healing.

> While I still consider myself a cessationist, the last few years have shown me that my spiritual life had gotten off track—that somehow, I along with many others in my theological tradition, have learned to do without the third person of the Trinity. . . . It is our prayer that this volume will be a stimulus to move other cessationists to take more seriously the ministry of the Holy Spirit today. In short, we are asking a fundamental question that all cessationists must ask themselves: "If the Holy Spirit did not die in the first century, what in the world is he doing today?" . . . As a cessationist, I can affirm the fact of present-day miracles without affirming the miracle-worker. God is still a God of healing even though I think his normal modus operandis is not through a faith-healer. . . . At the same time, the problem with many non-charismatics is that although they claim that God can heal, they act as if he won't. We often don't believe in God's ability—we don't really believe that God can heal.[5]

So, cessationist or not, we can surely all agree that the Western church should increase its hunger for and experience of answered prayer, the ability to discern the Lord's guidance, and the supernatural power of God's kingdom.

Second, philosophers of science make a distinction that may be of help in the present context. Regarding the question of whether a given scientific theory is a rational one, philosophers have broken down this issue into two sorts of rationality: the rationality of acceptance and the rationality of pursuit. The former refers to the fact that a given theory has adequate confirmation to warrant scientists to accept or believe the theory. The latter refers to the fact that it is rational for scientists to pursue testing, experimenting with and trying to confirm a particular theory. Here's the key point: *It can be rational to pursue a theory even if it is not yet rational to accept it.*

This could happen when a theory new to scientists holds promise or is being recommended by prominent scientists in the field, even if the theory has not yet achieved the status of being so well justified that one should believe it is true. By way of application, even if you have not personally experienced much of God's miraculous power (or at least you are unaware of having experienced it), and even if you have spent your Christian life in churches whose achievements can largely be explained by human organization and skill, it may still be most sensible for you to seek to learn about and hear of God's interventions for his children today.

To put the point differently, even if deep in our hearts we are skeptical about the power of prayer or the reality of contemporary, supernatural manifestations of the power of God, it may still be the most reasonable thing we could do to seek to learn of such things. Though we cannot directly change our beliefs by will alone (as discussed in chapter one), we can change them indirectly, and one important means is by seeking to expose ourselves to accounts of God's miraculous actions for his children. Thus, it may be rational for one to pursue growth and exposure to these things even if one is not yet in a position to say he or she is rationally justified in believing that these things still happen.

But how does one go about this in light of the sources of skepticism listed above? In our journey, there is one principle we learned from Chuck Kraft that has greatly deepened our trust and confidence in God: the principle of the *credible witness*.[6] A credible witness is someone we trust who is stable, reliable and informed enough to be qualified to testify to something, who has no reason to lie or exaggerate, and who is respected in the broader Christian community or among those whom you know well.

You will have to judge if we are, for you, credible witnesses. Even if we end up not functioning that way for you, we hope to stimulate you to seek to hear similar things from people who *could* function as credible witnesses for you. In the section to follow, we'll share various experiences we hope will illustrate the power of testimony to build God-confidence. What if a believer tried more wholeheartedly to rely on the incredible promises of Jesus (mentioned in chapter four), what might it look like in contemporary life? With God as our witness, we give you our word that what we are about to share is the truth and the whole truth with no exaggeration. We have selected experiences—from our own lives or from the lives of those we know well enough to vouch for—that actually happened. Note that if two of us have seen happen such things to follow, can you imagine how incredibly active God is today if even only a tenth of all Christians in the world today have had such encounters?

Six Areas of God-Confidence-Building Testimony

1. "Ordinary" answers to prayer. In the early months after my conversion, I (J. P.) learned a lesson about answered prayer that has stayed with me for thirty-five years. It is an event that happened to me at the beginning of my ministry.[7] In 1971 I was assigned to work with Campus Crusade for Christ at a college campus in Golden, Colorado (suburb of Denver). I began to pray specifically that God would provide my roommate and me with a white house with a white picket fence around a grassy front yard approximately two to three miles from campus, costing no more than $115 per month (this was 1971!). I hoped such a place would provide a sense of home for times of ministry and meetings with our students. After two weeks of daily prayer for this, I arrived in Golden and looked for three days for a place to live. I must have seen fifteen different places. I found nothing at all in Golden, but there was a two-bedroom apartment ten miles away in Denver for $130 per month. Frustrated, I told the manager I would take it. She informed me that the apartment was the only one left. A couple had seen it that morning, and had that day to make their decision. If they did not take it, it was mine. I called her around five o'clock that evening and learned that the couple had moved in. I was back to square one.

That evening, I received a phone call from a fellow Crusade staff member, Kaylon Carr. No one, not even my roommate, knew anything at all about my prayer request. Kaylon asked if I still needed a place to live and proceeded to tell me that that very day she had gone to Denver Seminary, looked on their bulletin board, and spotted a pastor who wanted to rent a house in Golden to Christians. I met the pastor at the house the next morning around nine o'clock. I drove up to a white house with a white picket fence surrounding a grassy front yard that was two miles from campus and rented for $110 per month! Ray Womack and I lived there for the year and had a home to which we could invite students for ministry. By meditating on this, I have strengthened over and over again my faith to believe God.

A couple of years ago during a class on Christian spirituality, I (Klaus) was teaching at Talbot School of Theology. Each week we would pray for one student, standing around him or her and praying as a group, praying as the Spirit would lead us. One of the students in the class, Jason Lanker, was in his second semester of doctoral studies. Jason and his wife, Heather, had asked God to provide for his tuition bills, as an indication of God's guidance to go back to school. "That way," he said "if the finances ever dried up, I would know that he was leading me in a different direction." But when the second semester arrived Jason was still short of funds. So Jason began praying for God to provide the exact amount of his tuition bill, $2,117.60, which was due by the coming Friday. But on Friday no funds arrived. Jason was flabbergasted. "How could the God who had made his will so clear just one semester before have left me out in the cold? My disbelief was palpable, and by Monday morning the anger that had been brewing all weekend boiled over in a two-day tirade against God."

Tuesday evening was the doctoral class. When the time came, class members gathered around Jason, and we prayed for him, including his request for money to pay his tuition bill. On the ride home from class, Jason's heart began to turn from anger to brokenness, enough to hear God's voice. God reminded Jason that Jason had set up the arrangement about finances coming in as an indication for continued doctoral studies. But instead of accepting God's answer, Jason was upset. It was a reminder to look for God's way, and not be distracted by the particular path he happened to be on at the moment.

On Wednesday evening, Heather was looking through some letters that her senile grandmother had written to her but had never mailed. Heather's father had accidentally found these letters as he was rummaging through some piles of old correspondence at his mother's (her grandmother's) house. To her amazement, included in the many letters with expressions of love for her were a number of bank bonds. After all the bonds had been tallied, they totaled $2,000! When they deposited the bonds in the bank the next day, the bank receipt reported the figure of $2,117.60! The bonds had appreciated. As Jason looked at the receipt bearing that specific amount, tears began to flow in response to the miraculous provision from God, and the guidance to remain in doctoral studies.

A few years ago my family and I (J. P.) were hit with an unexpected financial crisis. Shortly thereafter during a morning walk I told the Lord that I was at a point where I really needed to see him intervene for me. Suddenly, a thought came to me: "Why don't you ask me to do something for you now?" I wasn't sure it was the Lord or my own thoughts, but I responded to what I thought was his prompting and asked that he bring my family a specific amount of money that very day. My faith was not particularly strong at this time. The mail came and went with no check. But at 5:20 that evening, completely out of the blue and totally unexpected, I received an amount *above what I had requested* from someone who knew me but knew nothing of my situation. It was simply incredible, and besides the wonderful provision from God, this answer to prayer engendered God-confidence in my entire family and me.

These incidents listed may seem fairly small and insignificant. In one sense, they are. After all, getting a rental house or receiving specific amounts of money as an answer to prayer is not as important as world peace. But an answer to that global request is hard to measure, and, in any case, the incidents seemed big at the moment to those who were praying. And these answers to prayer show that God does care about the so-called small things of daily life. As an example, here's a moving account given to me by a doctor friend of mine:

> Our daughter, Ashley, who was probably about ten years old at the time, had two parakeets. One of them had just died. She told her mother that she wanted to get another one so that she would have a couple again. Mother, however, had had enough pets for the time being and told Ashley that we weren't going to get another parakeet at this time. Ashley, however, had a mind of her own. She said that she was going to pray to God for another parakeet, which she did. The next day, Ashley was playing outside with her friends when one of the kids saw that there was a bird in the tree. They all knew that Ashley had just lost her pet. It was a parakeet, the same color as the one she had just lost! (To this point, no one could remember ever having found a parakeet in the neighborhood before—and this occurred just the next day.) You can imagine her sense of triumph as she brought the bird home and announced that God had answered her prayer.

My doctor friend shared the sense of utter surprise and awe that he and his wife experienced as Ashley brought an exact duplicate of her lost parakeet into the house the next day, carrying the bird on her finger! Ponder something with us for a moment. How could an unbeliever explain this away? It would stretch all credibility to claim that this was just a happy coincidence. When was the last time you heard of a parakeet flying around in someone's backyard, one which looked exactly like their deceased pet, one which came the very next day after their pet died, one which came the very next day after a family member specifically asked God for a new parakeet, and one which allowed a little girl to capture it and bring it into the house!

2. Incredible providential "coincidences." Sometimes God orchestrates a convergence of factors at just the right moment to meet a need. I (Klaus) have sensed that God was calling me to a season of writing, but one always wonders if that is just a reflection of personal preferences or if God also affirms that direction. One particular day about a year ago I received encouraging comments from four different persons about four different writing projects—two books already published and two books I was still in the process of writing. Three came in the morning (an e-mail from a colleague, an encouraging comment from my wife after reading a draft of a chapter— she counts, too, though she's refreshingly biased—and a phone call from a friend informing me that my book *Wasting Time with God* had ministered to a friend of theirs). A fourth comment arrived that evening from J. P. about our first book, *The Lost Virtue of Happiness*, which Larry Crabb, speaking at an evangelical seminary presidents' gathering, had mentioned as having ministered to him. By the time I received the third comment, I knew this was no coincidence but that God was piling up affirmations so I would notice and be encouraged. That was a great day of affirmation.

A few summers ago I (J. P.) suffered from a series of anxiety attacks that led to a debilitating seven-month depression.[8] Almost immediately after sinking into an emotional and spiritual abyss, I began to be plagued with doubts and self-criticism about my academic, scholarly work. My self-talk, which I believe was energized by demonic attacks, was filled with repeated accusations that I had wasted my life studying, writing, and lecturing, and that my intellectual endeavors for the cause of Christ had achieved very little. This repeated thought plagued me for several weeks, plunging me deeper into depression. I felt my work had been meaningless and, as a result, that my whole life was basically meaningless. In the midst of this plunge, I went to Columbia International University in Columbia, South Carolina, to deliver a five-day lecture series. I live in Southern California, and South Carolina seems halfway around the world to me. I knew no one in Columbia and had never been there before.

Just before dinner on July 15, 2003, I came down with an extreme migraine headache. I can go five years without even a small headache, so this was a first for me. I took Tylenol, canceled my evening lecture and went to bed in my dorm room at Columbia International. But things got worse. My head was wracked with pain. Around six o'clock I received a phone call from a conferee who lived in the area. He said he was taking me to the emergency room. I slumped into his front seat, and he drove me to a walk-in clinic about fifteen to twenty miles away in Irmo, South Carolina. I staggered in, left my driver's license at the front desk and was whisked away to the emergency room. Immediately, two nurses hooked monitors to my chest and brain, and began testing me to find out what was wrong. My blood pressure was off the charts. They gave me an injection to alleviate the headache, and it began to work quickly.

After about five minutes of this, the doctor on call that evening walked in the door. Holding my driver's license he said, "Are you J. P. Moreland? The one who teaches at Talbot Seminary?" Taken a bit off-guard, I nodded. "I don't believe this! There are nurses here who would give their eye teeth if a movie star walked through those doors. In my case, if I could pick one person in the entire country to come in here, it would be you. Dr. Moreland, I can't thank you enough for what you have done in the intellectual world for the cause of Christ! I have read almost all your books, and, hey, you know that book *Body and Soul* you wrote with Scott Rae? I teach ethics at a local community college, and I use that as a text. I can't believe I am getting to meet you!"

It turned out that I had most likely eaten some bad shrimp at dinner the day before this happened, and it takes about twenty-four hours for the food poisoning to hit someone. But as soon as this doctor shared with me the impact I had had on him, the Lord spoke to me: "I am well pleased with your academic work for my name's sake. You have done well. Keep trusting me." At the very moment of my need to be reassured of the meaning of my intellectual work, I met a doctor who "happened" to be on duty that evening in a city in which I had never been who valued the very work for which I needed consolation during my depression. What a "coincidence"! It has been my repeated meditation on things like this in my own life that has reassured me that God knows about my needs and that I can trust him to act when he knows the timing is right.

There are a couple of ways to recognize whether such events are really from God. The more two factors are present, the more grounds you have for being confident that a circumstance is, indeed, from the hand of God and not merely a coincidence: (1) the more improbable the event, the more likely it is from God; (2) the greater the specificity and religious significance of the event, the more likely it is from God. The first principle is pretty obvious. If I pray that the sun will come up tomorrow and it does, it is quite unlikely that my prayer had anything to do with the result. The sun would have come up even if I had not prayed. If I pray to get a place to live in the next twelve months and it happens, then even though God may very well have answered this prayer, because the outcome is fairly probable, the result does not provide much by way of evidence for answered prayer. However, if I pray for a white house with a white picket fence two miles from campus with a rent of no more that $115 per month and it happens, this result is highly improbable.

James Rutz tells of the distinguished Indian evangelist Sadhu Chellappa who, while on a mission trip to a village north of Midras, was awakened in the middle of the night by what seemed to be God's voice telling him, *Leave this house quickly and run away!*[9] Chellappa quickly dressed and obeyed, running into the darkness with no directions for where to go. As he passed beneath a large tree, he sensed the Lord telling him to stop and begin to preach. He was in the middle of nowhere and, due to the darkness, could not detect anyone within listening distance. But he started to preach anyway. When he reached the point of giving a gospel invitation, he was surprised to hear a voice from the top of the tree and to see a man climbing down. As it turned out, the man in the tree right above the preaching Chellappa had gone out in the middle of the night to hang himself. Instead, he tearfully received Christ. Clearly, this was no coincidence! If Chellappa had merely passed a stranger on the street that night, or simply run into a big tree, since such a thing is highly probable, it would not raise as much as a suspicion that God was involved.

Chellappa's story illustrates the second piece of advice. Improbable things happen every day. But when something improbable takes place that has a very special religious significance, then we are on safe grounds to see God's intervention in the occurrence. The salvation of the suicidal man is clearly of great biblical significance because the Great Shepherd is like that—leaving the ninety-nine to save the one lost sheep. If Chellappa had improbably run into a passing stranger who was looking for a Snickers bar, which neither had any special religious significance for the stranger nor was something Chellappa could supply, then the event would most likely be just a coincidence. Contrast this with the parakeet incident involving the doctor friend and his daughter. What makes this "little" event religiously significant was that a prayer was offered for this specific outcome, and a little girl's need was met and her God-confidence increased (not to mention that of her parents!).

So if something happens for which one has prayed or which meets a need at just the right moment, then the event has special significance in the context of one's life as a disciple. The combination of improbability and special significance may not be necessary to spot a loving act of God—after all, he can do the probable and expected if he wants to—but it is sufficient. We build our faith on acts of our loving God if (but not only if) they conform to these conditions.

3. *Miraculous healing*. We have both seen and heard eyewitness testimony to miraculous healings too numerous to mention. During the last two years, in our church alone, there have been at least six cases of cancer miraculously healed, some of them terminal and beyond medical intervention; one person who instantly had her complete eyesight restored from significant, partial blindness after receiving prayer; a Vietnam veteran blinded in one eye for twenty-five years by a grenade explosion who received full sight after being prayed for by a team of several people; and a young deaf boy who miraculously received full hearing after a friend of ours laid hands on him and prayed. These stories are real—in most cases we know the people involved in praying—and they could be multiplied many times over by other examples of miraculous healing.

Not long ago, one of my graduate students came to see me during my office hours at the university. His name is Nathan, and he is an extremely bright young man. As he recalled what God had done for him, tears came to his eyes, and as I listened in amazement, my eyes filled with tears as well. Nathan told me that when he was thirteen years old he was diagnosed with GERDS (gastroesophageal reflux disease), in which the valve between his esophagus and stomach did not work properly. He would wake up every night gasping for breath and choking. He could not breathe because of the stomach acid that had gathered in his chest and the severe pain that resulted. Consequently, Nathan developed insomnia; he had to sleep sitting up and did not sleep through the night one single time for nine years. In 2002, Nathan got married, and his wife urged him to go to a doctor to investigate surgery. He did and was told that he would need a series of five surgeries and would be on medication the rest of his life. Even then, the doctor said, he would be only about 90 percent healed.

The next day, Nathan and his wife went to a small group Bible study they regularly attended. That evening a missionary couple from Thailand shared about their ministry, a ministry that included miraculous healings. No one at the Bible study knew of Nathan's illness. Before leaving for the study, Nathan expressed to his wife that he was skeptical about the missionary couple, even though he had no good reason for his skepticism. However, in spite of his skepticism, he went to the study that night. And something incredible and shocking took place. In Nathan's own words, "During the Bible study, out of the blue, the speaker stopped praying for another person, turned and said, 'someone in the room is suffering from gastroesophageal reflux disease.' This man had never met me nor could he have known the disease name." Nathan then told me that the missionary described a very painful event that had happened between the person with GERDS (Nathan had not yet identified himself as the person) and his father when he was diagnosed with the disease as a young boy (all details of which were unknown to anyone, including Nathan's wife, and were completely accurately described). Nathan raised his hand to identify himself as the person with GERDS. When he did so, the missionary came to him, laid hands on him and prayed for his healing. As emotion welled up within him, Nathan relayed to me that at that very moment he was instantly and completely healed! From that night until the present (about three full years), Nathan has never had an incident, he has slept through every night since that Bible study (he hadn't done this for nine years), and the doctor cleared Nathan shortly thereafter of the diagnosis. I met Nathan's wife a few weeks ago at a student gathering, and without warning I pulled her aside to ask about the incident. She confirmed every detail of the story to me.[10]

What a wonderful and living God we serve! We hope these true, credible accounts fill your own heart with trust and confidence in a God who is there. And God is there whether or not he chooses to heal. We seek his care and trust him whatever the outcome. When we hear stories like these, our response should not be, Why doesn't this happen to me? For one thing, you never know what God will do for you in the future, since the "already" phase of Jesus' kingdom has come and his promises invite us all to try them out. But more importantly, these powerful testimonies are designed to build your confidence in the triune God and his Word. Allow these accounts to have this effect on your heart and mind as you meditate on them.

4. What happens when Jesus shows up? In addition to Holy Scripture, the living God still communicates to his children and to those who don't know him in ways that are supernatural. In chapter six, we'll take some time to offer the biblical basis for this kind of divine guidance; now we'll just share the stories. When these sorts of things happen, they have a tremendous impact on building the God-confidence of those involved and of those who hear about them.[11]

In the last ten years, more Muslims have come to Christ than in the previous thousand years. And reports from numerous missions agencies say that many conversions come from the Lord Jesus himself or an angel directly appearing in the extramental world or in a vision or dream to individuals or entire villages. In a recent newsletter from Campus Crusade's Jesus Film Project, Jim Green—a highly respected Crusade staffer for forty years—reports that if you were to gather a typical group of one hundred new converts from Islam and ask them how they first learned of Jesus, ninety-nine of them would say, "I saw Him in a vision. He appeared in brilliant white light and told me that He was the Way and that I was to seek Him out."[12] When missionaries find such people, they have the joy of explaining more fully the gospel of the Lord Jesus. One of several incidents reported by Green is worth noting:

> The next report comes from a traveling "JESUS" film team that was working in one of these countries. The team was driving through a remote, dangerous region that had hardly been touched by the good news. A policeman flagged down the team's car which was filled with 16mm projection equipment and gospel literature. The policeman asked the team to give a ride to an Islamic teacher who immediately got in. You can imagine their anxiety when this highly respected teacher asked, *"Tell me, are you the ones planning to tell people about God?"* Entrusting themselves to the Lord, they responded, *"Yes, we are."* Astonishment followed. Bouncing along the dusty road the teacher told the team how he had experienced a vision, a unique dream. *"I was told to come to this spot in the road, at this time, that I would encounter someone who would tell me about God. It must be you."*[13]

Eyewitness accounts like this could be multiplied over and over again. A few months ago a friend of ours was talking with a missionary, a representative of Missionary Aviation Fellowship, who worked with Muslims in Indonesia. Our friend asked the missionary whether he had ever seen such manifestations of Jesus and angels. With a grin on his face, he reported that, indeed, several such occurrences had happened to those to whom he had ministered. In fact, just two weeks earlier he had worn a blue sports jacket to the marketplace to get vegetables and a Muslim stranger approached him. In a dream the previous night, the Muslim man had been instructed by an angel to go to the marketplace, approach a man wearing a blue sports jacket and ask him about God. In the dream he had actually seen the missionary's face, so he was certain about what to do. The missionary led the man to Jesus Christ right on the spot!

Supernatural events like these are happening all over the world, but they also happen quite regularly in this country, and they are not always connected to evangelism. In fact, most of the time when God speaks through impressions; a still, small voice; a dream or vision; or a word from a person, the purpose is guidance, encouragement, edification, the softening of a hard heart, assurance that God does indeed know about one's trials and is near in the midst of them, and the strengthening of God-confidence.

Last year Brian, a close friend of ours, was invited to speak on the supernatural nature of God's kingdom in a class at a local Christian university. I (J. P.) came along as a visitor. There were seven professors in attendance and about fifty graduate and undergraduate students. During the second hour of the class, after lecturing for about fifteen minutes, Brian paused and began to pray silently for a moment. He then singled out a professor, Dr. Johnson (not the person's real name), attending the class that evening, someone he did not know although they had been briefly introduced along with a dozen or so folks before the session started. In front of the class Brian shared that the professor had five heart desires that were being brought before the Lord in prayer and that God was about to fulfill all of them. Brian specifically identified all five desires, and they were quite specific. I could see the professor begin to tremble and cry a bit in response to Brian's words. The incident lasted about two minutes, and Brian returned to lecturing.

After the lecture, I took the professor aside and asked what had happened. Dr. Johnson's response put the fear of God in my heart. This word to the professor had occurred in the second hour following a class break. Just prior to the second half of class, during the break in a quiet area outside the classroom, the professor had privately expressed these specific five heart desires to Jesus. They were exactly the five Brian had spoken about. In fact, Dr. Johnson was praying for a specific concern at the exact moment Brian began sharing these heart desires in the classroom. Brian's first word was the very concern being prayed for at the time! And people think God doesn't reveal things to his children today! I spoke to the professor about two months later. These personal words given by Brian had incredibly edified Dr. Johnson. A sustained intimacy with the Father had been birthed at that moment deep within by God's voice through Brian.

But there's more. After the class and in the presence of one of the professors, the most vocal, skeptical student in the class came up to Brian and expressed his doubts about such words of guidance. He then told Brian that during the class he sensed that Brian had something to say to him, and he was curious about whether he had sensed correctly. Brian acknowledged the student's intuition and said he had not felt free to speak to the student in front of the class for fear of embarrassing him. When asked by the student what he was going to say, Brian proceeded to tell the student that the Lord had told him that the night before the student and his wife had experienced a terrible argument. Brian went on to state specifically what the topic of their argument had been, and he then spoke words of encouragement to the student about repenting and seeking the Lord's love for his wife. The student wilted. In fact, not only was Brian right about the argument, but he also was precisely correct about the specific source of disagreement! The student walked away a believer in such words of guidance, and, more importantly, he left with a deep hunger to know and obey the Lord. When Brian told me about this, I called the professor who had witnessed the event. The professor is a traditional evangelical in his theological orientation, and he confirmed to me the details I have just shared with you.

So that our intentions are clear, we reiterate something we said earlier in this chapter: Our purpose in sharing these stories is not to provide guidance in hearing God's voice or in explaining why God is sometimes silent or why some people hear him more easily than others or why God answers some prayers and doesn't answer others. Our purpose is to remind us that Christianity is actually true. The Christian God is really there, and he is not silent! He is worthy of our growing confidence in him and his Word!

5. Touched by an angel. The unseen supernatural world is a realm of innumerable spirit beings—angels and demons—who interact with us in countless ways, from subtle, easy-to-ignore ways to overt, clear manifestations of their presence. We know many credible, honest people who have encountered angels and demons in various circumstances. The combined weight of their testimony has brought both of us to the point that we simply cannot doubt the reality of angels and demons even if we wanted to. The biblical teaching about this realm is, as always, right on the money.

In September 2005 an amazing event happened to me (J. P). To feel the force of the story, I have to start in the fall of 2004. On a weekend in October 2004, I flew to Seattle to speak at a weekend retreat for a traditional, noncharismatic Bible church. After my second talk, a woman approached me somewhat sheepishly and asked to speak with me in private. I agreed, and with some hesitation she said that for about a half an hour during my talk she had clearly seen three angels guarding me as I spoke (one was on each side, and a taller one was behind me looking over my head at the audience). When she left, I asked four or five people, including the pastor, to tell me about the woman, and to a person they said she was probably the most spiritually mature woman in the congregation. Still, I was a skeptical of her claim, but I retained her testimony in my heart.

Fast forward to September 2005. While I lay praying on my bed one night as I pondered some deep burdens in my heart, I said something to the Lord I had never prayed in my life. I asked him to do two things: Send the three angels back to protect me during this intense period of special burdens (I told him that since I don't see such things, for all I knew they were already around me, but just in case, I asked God to send them back) and somehow let me know that they are there. I continued praying for about another twenty minutes and then drifted off to sleep. I was about to experience the shock of my life.

Less than a week later I received an e-mail (which I kept) from a philosophy graduate student named Mark who was taking a metaphysics class with me that semester. Mark began by saying that he had wanted to share something with me for a few days, but he wanted to process it with two or three other graduate students before he did. It turns out that a few days earlier during one of my lectures, he had seen three angels standing in the room (one on each side, a taller one behind me) for five to ten minutes before they disappeared! I asked Mark to come to my office, and a few days later we talked further. Because he respected me as his professor, he began by saying that he would never want to say anything to me that he wasn't sure of, and he knew that the angels were next to me in the room and not in his head. In fact, he gave me a sketch he had drawn from his angle of perception in the class, a sketch of me and the angels (which I kept).

I checked out his story with the other students, and they confirmed that he had told them of this encounter days before sending me the e-mail. Besides a possible encounter as a little boy, Mark had never seen an angel in his life and was not prone to such things. When I told him about my prayer request of a few days earlier, his mind was blown! So was mine! Mark, a credible graduate student not prone to angelic visions, had seen as I lectured three—not two or four, but three—angels standing around me in the precise position the lady had described months earlier. And I found out about this within a few days of praying for the first time in my life to have the three angels sent back and for God to somehow let me know about it. I have not seen them myself, but I cannot doubt their presence. Madonna may think we live in a material world, and Carl Sagan may have opined that the physical cosmos was all there ever was, is or will be, but they are dead, dead wrong. We live in a supernatural world indeed![14]

6. *Satan's kingdom and demonic spirits.* Whether or not we like it, demons are very real and constitute part of the unseen supernatural world. One of Jesus' purposes for his incarnation was to destroy the works of the devil (Hebrews 2:14-15; 1 John 3:8). And one way he diminished Satan's kingdom and brought in the kingdom of God was by casting out demons (Matthew 12:26, 28). We Westerners readily accept psychological explanations for a wide range of phenomena— for example, multiple personality disorders and schizophrenia—and we are correct in doing so. But we would be foolish and quite naive to fail to avail ourselves of spiritual-warfare principles and appeals to demonization when circumstances warrant it. Our purpose here is not to provide detailed teaching about demonization and its recognition.[15] Thus, we will have to be content with two brief points. First, Christians and non-Christians alike can be oppressed and harmed by demons to one degree or another (e.g., Ephesians 4:26-27; James 3:15). Second, when at least one of three criteria is satisfied, then one is justified in believing a demon is present: (1) the alleged demonized person cannot do things that Scripture says cannot be done by a demon (e.g., confess Jesus as Lord); (2) during a deliverance session, the person expresses private (usually embarrassing) details of the life of someone in the prayer team, details that the demonized person simply could not have known; and (3) overt physical phenomena such as moving objects are present.

As we said above, demons are real indeed. A few years ago, a Biola University undergraduate began to experience sudden and unexpected episodes of a racing heart. The episodes were so severe that she would pass out on the spot, sometimes in the middle of class.

She saw several doctors, underwent various tests, and no cause was found, so she wore a heart monitor to enable the doctors to gather more data on her condition. Desperate for help, the student and a friend visited the office of Biola professor Clint Arnold. Dr. Arnold is a world-renowned New Testament scholar, and he is an authority on demons. Dr. Arnold told me that when the girls entered his office, he clearly sensed an evil presence. He offered a deliverance prayer, all three sensed the malevolent spirit's departure, and the girl was instantly healed of the condition on the spot. It never returned. The incident was so incredible that it was reported in the Biola University student newspaper.[16]

Another friend of mine, whom I'll call Dr. Smith, received his Ph.D. from one of the top ten universities in America, has published a technical monograph with what may be the top academic publisher in the world, and teaches at a well-respected university. Dr. Smith lives alone, and he told me recently that for a period of two months (which ended about two months ago as of this writing) he had seen overt demonic phenomena in his condominium. It began with a specific piece of furniture moving in his living room, an event he witnessed with his own eyes. Next, his phone began to ring repeatedly with no one on the line. Shortly thereafter, when he went downstairs for breakfast, he found a large wreath which had been hanging on his wall lying in the middle of the floor about twelve feet from the wall as though someone had tossed it over there. No one had entered his home during the night, nor does Dr. Smith walk in his sleep. Finally, he has discovered pictures in his bedroom turned around 180 degrees from their ordinary position, and no one (at least no human) could have done this. Dr. Smith has lived in his home for eight years, and nothing has ever happened like this until a friend came to stay with him. The phenomena began a few weeks before the friend's arrival, lasted for the two weeks of his stay, and continued for a few weeks after his departure. Frustrated and frightened, Dr.

Smith enlisted the help of a prayer team from his church who came and prayed over each room in his home. As of this writing, since that time the manifestations have ceased.

These two incidents involve highly educated, credible people who are not hysterical, gullible or liars. Additionally, in the most recent edition of our university's alumni publication, *Biola Connections,* there is a featured story on demons.[17] The story contains interviews with six professors, all of whom have Ph.D.s in their respective fields. All have witnessed demonic phenomena, including flying objects at a home plagued by demons, supernatural knowledge, induced nausea and an oppressive sense of evil.

We share this to remind you that reality is not exhausted by what you can detect with your five senses. The spiritual world and spiritual warfare are absolutely real, make no mistake about it. And let this reminder not only strengthen your God-confidence—for "the one who is in you is greater than the one who is in the world" (1 John 4:4)—but also give you a renewed sense of urgency to be involved in the conflict for the hearts and minds of people the world over.

Conclusion

We acknowledge that this chapter has been unbalanced in this sense: We have not shared much about times of dryness in which God seems absent and inactive, and we have not shared times when our prayers have not been answered.[18] We all experience such times, and it is important to learn how to grow in them. But this has not been our purpose. Our goal has been to exhort, explain and illustrate the God-confidence-building power of bearing witness to the supernatural manifestations of God and angels. In our thirty-five years of ministry, we have seen repeatedly how trust drains away if one comes to believe that God no longer interacts with his people and manifests himself in overtly supernatural ways. We are told by the secular elites that the universe is religiously ambiguous—no one can know whether God is real, nor can we know what he is like if he is actually there. The universe runs day by day, we are told, in utter silence from the supernatural realm, if there even really is one. God, it seems, stopped acting with the death of the last apostle.

As academics ourselves, we reject these claims. Consider the events recalled in this chapter. They were drawn from our own lives, the lives of our close friends and the lives of those in our local church. Now, multiply our little church by tens upon tens of thousands of other churches, and you will get a feel for how miracles are literally daily occurrences in America. Multiply that by the events occurring today around the world, and we see that ours is not merely the "visited planet"; it's the constantly revisited planet! No wonder researcher James Rutz exclaims, "Since about the mid-1980s, a tide of miracles has begun to engulf the entire planet. As time goes on, miracles are multiplying like loaves and fishes."[19]

One reason people don't know about these matters is that they do not share miracle stories with others when they experience them. But if this chapter strengthened your God-confidence, we urge you to seek and give credible witness to God's supernatural kingdom. Keep a journal in which you record prayers that were answered. In fact, we encourage you to try out a prayer project, petitioning God for a need for another or for yourself, bringing the matter before the Lord several times during the day for the next three days. Ask the Lord what to pray for, and see how God leads you in this prayer project.

Connect with others and ask them to share the things they have seen and heard. Provide a regular place in your weekly church program for such things to happen. Read credible books which recount such things.[20] Paul once remarked that the miraculous events surrounding Jesus and his kingdom has not been "done in a corner" (Acts 26:26). Neither are they done in a corner today. It's important for us to come out of the closet and give witness to a living God who acts. In the next chapter, we'll continue sharing more stories of

God encounters, as we explore one area in which we all want God's leading—seeking God's guidance.

> *Faith, in the sense in which I am here using the word,*
> *is the art of holding on to things your reason has once accepted,*
> *in spite of your changing moods. For moods will change, whatever*
> *view your reason takes. I know that by experience. . . .*
> *That is why Faith is such a necessary virtue: unless you teach*
> *your moods "where they get off," you can never be either a sound*
> *Christian or even a sound atheist, but just a creature dithering*
> *to and fro, with its beliefs really dependent on the weather*
> *and the state of its digestion.*
>
> C. S. LEWIS, *MERE CHRISTIANITY*

Questions for Personal Reflection or Group Discussion

1. At the beginning of this chapter, the authors claimed that the chief source of doubt among Americans is "God's apparent inactivity, indifference or impotence in the face of tragedy and suffering." Do you agree or disagree with this claim? Why or why not? Can you think of specific examples from the media or your own life that support or dispute this claim?

2. On pages 134-35, the authors discussed the role of regular testimony (i.e., witnessing) about God's great acts in the lives of the Israelites. In your own words, describe why you think regularly remembering the great acts of God is important in a life marked by God-confidence.

3. In your journal or in your small group, pause for a moment to take an inventory of your thoughts and reactions to the stories the authors shared in this chapter. Were you skeptical about the validity

of these stories? Did you find them encouraging? Why do you think you responded as you did?

4. Take a moment to consider the ways that God has intervened in your own life. Write them down in your journal or share them in your small group. Discuss a couple of ways you can begin to regularly share these stories with others to encourage them in their walk with God.

6

LEARNING TO TRUST IN GOD
FOR GUIDANCE ABOUT LIFE DECISIONS

In this book we've talked about various aspects of God-confidence. In part one of the book, we explained what it is and what are some of the barriers to increasing our trust in God. Faith is actually rooted in knowledge—a true belief about reality based on adequate grounds or an accurate experiential awareness of reality. Thus, faith is never opposed to reason or evidence when everything is taken into account. Biblical faith is not a blind leap in the dark. Although we don't have direct control to increase our God-confidence, we do have *indirect* control of the process. We can intend to change a belief over time (e.g., through meditation, study) by becoming aware of more evidence for the belief. Trust is fundamental to all personal relationships. Of course, our confidence in God is the most fundamental relationship.

Regarding barriers to trusting in God, in chapters one and two we identified two kinds of doubt and offered some practical steps to deal with each: (a) doubt that stems from seeing the world through Western cultural plausibility structures and (b) doubt regarding specific intellectual issues. Furthermore, we noted that we are also affective beings. Although we may think and believe, we mainly run our life from our thoughts and cognitions; in actuality our strongest emotions and desires usually guide us in all we do. Thus we thought it important to address this topic in chapter three and explore further how past emotional wounds can hinder our openness to trusting in others, including trust in God.

In part two of the book, our focus has been on increasing our expectations of God, building a case for how our God-confidence can grow. We have examined Jesus' amazing promises regarding God's desire to intervene in our lives at our request (e.g., "If you remain in me and my words remain in you, ask whatever you wish, and it will be given you," John 15:7). Through his teaching, and his own example of living dependently on God, Jesus is offered as a vision, painting a picture of what a life fully lived in God's kingdom looks like. Each believer has the opportunity to grow further into this reality in which, according to Jesus' teaching, more answers to prayer can be received than we are currently experiencing.

But some may wonder, are there indications of this kind of supernatural lifestyle in the contemporary world? According to sociologist Christian Smith, a chief source of doubt comes from God's apparent inactivity in the lives of people in the face of tragedy and suffering. We think what has been missing is Christians' willingness to share their supernatural encounters with God—witnessing to others about the amazing acts of God in their lives. Since we think hearing such stories can greatly build our God-confidence, the last chapter was filled with encouraging divine encounters, portraying some of the varied ways God has intervened in the lives of his children.

So then, how can we take active steps to grow in our reliance on God? In this final chapter we identify one important area for growing in our trust in God: seeking personal guidance from God for decision making about our future. We want to live in ways that are pleasing to God. How do we become aware of God's perspective on a particular decision we have to make? Can we be assured that God is directing our paths? Furthermore, once God has made his perspective known, are we willing to trust God's wisdom instead of what we think is best, when we want to decide differently? We hope to convey God's wonderful invitation to stretch our God-confidence so we can live more and more within the realm of his kingdom—living more by trust than by sight (2 Corinthians 5:7).

Asking for Guidance

Many years ago, God was pursuing Ken Eldred, a Stanford M.B.A. in his mid-thirties. Married, with a son, Ken and Roberta thought, *We owed our son the same opportunity to consider religion as we had been given, so he could come to his own decision about faith.*[1] So they planned to attend a series of churches, starting with the one Ken had attended as a child. They never left that first one. Each Sunday Ken wrestled with God, not about God's existence but about what would be God's calling on his life. Being a Christian is what he wanted to be. But Ken also wanted to be a businessman, yet he was getting the idea through the sermons "that any serious Christian could only serve God as a pastor; a true follower of Jesus would lay down his career and go into preaching."[2] One day, Ken bowed before God in submission, willing to do *whatever* God wanted, even if that meant the pastoral ministry. Although his heart was for business, Ken asked God to change his heart to do whatever God wanted.

As Ken grew in his God-confidence, he realized God's calling was to serve God in business, working through the desires of Ken's heart (Psalm 37:4).[3] God just wanted to see if Ken was willing to give up everything for him. Ken became aware that serious Christians don't have to change careers in order to serve God. Meeting the needs of others through business "is a high calling from God, and it was *my* calling."[4] Ken continued to study Scripture and committed himself to letting his faith affect his workday week, "to do my business by the Book."[5] The next milestone was learning that God was interested in the very details of Ken's work, "that God desired to partner with me—that He cared about business outcomes and wanted me to ask Him for specific results—deepened the sense of business as my ministry."[6]

Ken sensed God's direction to start a business. With the counsel of a partner, he ventured into something fairly new at the time (the early 1970s): a mail-order catalog business to service the computer needs of small companies. Along with the business plan, Ken also decided he didn't want to work more than forty hours per week, to leave time for God and family. This decision prevented venture capitalists from funding the company (they expected up to sixty hours of weekly work), so family and friends offered investment loans for the initial $50,000 needed to start the company.

Of course, the first year of any business is always a constant struggle, and everything Ken owned (including personal loan guarantees) was in the business. Per-day sales were beginning to slide south, from $2,300 eventually to $2,100. Ken desperately needed guidance from God. Did God really call him to this particular business, or did God have another in mind, or should Ken actually go into the pastoral ministry? Ken and Roberta decided to ask God for a confirmation to continue with the company. Since the main focus was per-day sales, Roberta suggested, "How about we take God's perfect number seven. Let's trust God for a $7,000 sales day. And just so you don't think it's a chance event, we're going to pray for three $7,000 days!"[7] Ken was eager to ask, but had no idea how God would come through. During the first half of their ten-day prayer vigil, Ken was terrified, but kept pressing the request to receive direction from God. Then a sense of confidence came over Ken that God was big enough to guide his children. If God didn't bring this kind of sales day, God had something else better up his sleeve.

By the end of the prayer period, on a Sunday, both Ken and Roberta believed God would do this miracle, starting the very next day on Monday, despite the continual sliding of sales to $1,800. Monday morning in the customer representative's office, Ken announced it would be a $7,000 sales day! The customer rep was skeptical, but by the end of the day, that amount had come in. No employees had known of the prayer request, and none were walking with the Lord at the time. It was an impressive event. A $7,000 sales day occurred on the following two Mondays, and then sales returned to earlier levels, $2,000 a day. For many years Ken could point to those sales graphs as "three monuments to God."[8] Through this partnership with God, Ken not only learned that God wanted Ken in this particular company but also that Ken could trust God to provide, whether or not God might lead him away from that company at some future point.

Ken's story illustrates the matter of divine guidance. Of course, the details of each believer's life context is different, but the general point comes through: God welcomes us when we seek his guidance and present our prayer requests. Over and over the Bible teaches that God is trustworthy. Each of us will need to learn that for ourselves, experientially. Our God-confidence grows as we step out to learn how trustworthy to us our God is. God invites us to ask and to trust him. We hope this chapter will help increase your expectations that God will be faithful to his many promises, that if we draw near to him, God will draw near to us (James 4:8).

Seeking God's Will and Praying According to God's Will

Before we address the foundational theological issues related to seeking divine guidance, we first need to clarify the elusive phrase "God's will." Since we are seeking God's will, we need to know what "God's will" means. Clarifying the meaning involves a bit of a challenge since the main evangelical theological traditions make somewhat conflicting claims about God and his will based on different ways of explaining the biblical data about this matter. Those differences significantly affect how Christians are advised to go about seeking divine guidance and making prayer requests to God.[9] Our general concern about theological systems is that, when emphasizing (or overemphasizing) one particular biblical theme, other important themes clearly taught in Scripture may be deemphasized or even ignored. The hazard of theological speculation—of going beyond the biblical data to propose a resolution for a particular theological tension—is the possibility of overlooking and discounting other important biblical themes.

In biblical study and theology, we think it's better to be faithful to the scriptural text and allow the tension to remain. If we can't fully explain this tension, then just affirm both biblical teachings and let the mystery stand. For example, we agree with theologians Gordon Lewis and Bruce Demarest—their comment applies equally to seeking guidance: *"Any view of God's predestination or providence that keeps people from praying indicates something out of line with the Bible's teaching."*[10] Our presentation of divine guidance offers our best synthesis of seemingly contradictory ideas in Scripture, keeping in mind the other key factors in assessing truth: theological tradition, reasoning and experience.

Generally speaking, "God's will" refers to two broad categories: something related to God's desired overarching plan for history, or something related to a lifestyle of righteousness that pleases God. Note that these two broad categories partially overlap, but they are not the same since God has permitted evil in his plan, and evil is opposed to righteousness. God's plan is not always fully revealed in Scripture (Deuteronomy 29:29), but some of God's decrees are known (e.g., the death of Jesus, Acts 2:23; 4:27-28). Additional theological terms that relate to God's plan include God's *providence*, how God sustains his world and what actually happens, and God's *permissive will*, what God permits to take place but which does not please him in the sense that evil actions permitted are opposed to his righteousness (e.g., although God is not the author of evil, he permits evil as a part of his plan). But, God's will as God's plan is *not* what we're seeking guidance about. It's the other category of God's will that we seek—*how to live within the range of what pleases God*.

What is the kind of life that pleases God? God is in the process of creating believers "to be like God in true righteousness and holiness" (Ephesians 4:24). For example,

> *It is God's will* that you should be sanctified: that you should avoid sexual immorality; that each of you should learn to control his own body in a way that is holy and honorable, not in passionate lust like the heathen, who do not know God. (1 Thessalonians 4:3-5, emphasis added)

> Give thanks in all circumstances, for *this is God's will* for you in Christ Jesus. (1 Thessalonians 5:18, emphasis added)

It's this broad category that Jesus is talking about when he says, "For whoever does the will of my Father in heaven is my brother and sister and mother" (Matthew 12:50; also see Matthew 7:21). Living within God's righteous standard is God's will for us. This category is sometimes called God's *preceptive* (principled) or *moral* will to distinguish it from God's decretive (decreed) will or plan. The matter of guidance relates to making decisions within the wide range of activities that fit within God's moral and holy standards.

So within this sphere of God's righteous and holy ways, we have a lot of options for decision making: Should we live in this city or that one? Live in this apartment or house or that one? Take a job at that business or go into business for myself? We would like more specific guidance, which raises an underlying theological question.

Flexibility Within God's Plan?
Is there any flexibility for human choices within God's plan? Addressing this question is foundational to making any headway in stepping out in God-confidence to seek guidance. One way to analyze the issue is by talking about means and ends—for any given

goal or end to be accomplished there are means to accomplish that goal. Let's reframe the question to get to the nub of the issue: Is there always only one best means that God has in mind for you or me regarding each decision we make for the goals he has in mind for us? Or, in some cases, are there a variety of good options from which we could choose?

If it is the case that there is always only *one best* means to accomplish *every end* that God has in mind, then of course God needs to select every means, since only he knows what is best. But is there always only one best means? For example, does it really matter, for all eternity, whether I wear shoes that buckle up or have shoelaces or just slip on? Does it really matter, for all eternity, whether I eat cold cereal or toast or oatmeal for breakfast? Does it really matter, for all eternity, what make and model of car I drive or if I'm able to afford a car? Within life as we know it, it seems that there are arenas in which the particular means selected toward a goal has little or no eternal consequence.

An obscure passage in the Old Testament supports this idea that, in some cases, God is amenable to different means to accomplish an end. God wanted the prophet Ezekiel to present an acted parable. Ezekiel was supposed to eat barley cake cooked over human dung (Ezekiel 4:12), to which Ezekiel protested with great anxiety, "Not so, Sovereign LORD! I have never defiled myself" (Ezekiel 4:14). So God responded to Ezekiel's sensitivities, "'Very well,' [the LORD] said, 'I will let you bake your bread over cow manure instead of human excrement'" (Ezekiel 4:15). God permitted Ezekiel's preference for cow dung to stand over God's preference for human dung. The particular means used appears inconsequential to God's intentions.

Another example of this flexibility comes from an occasion when King David had sinned. He conducted a census of the people of Israel, which meant he was relying more on military might than on God's power. As part of the process, God offered David three possible measures of punishment from which David could choose. "Shall there come upon you three years of famine in your land? Or three months of fleeing from your enemies while they pursue you? Or three days of plague in your land?" (2 Samuel 24:13). If there were always only one best means, why would God offer David three possible punishments? The biblical data suggest two general categories of divine actions. In some cases, God *alone* determines the means, and Scripture records a divine *unconditional* statement, for which God never changes his mind (e.g., not to curse Israel, Numbers 23:19; the death of King David's infant, 2 Samuel 12:14). Yet in other cases, there is a range of good means for which God can grant a choice among good options. The following are a few examples.

Abraham was able to negotiate with God the standard for judging Sodom and Gomorrah from fifty righteous people down to ten righteous people. God was open to considering a lower standard of judgment, letting the cities remain for the sake of ten righteous people, instead of fifty. This was agreeable to God (Genesis 18:20-33; although, sadly, even ten righteous people could not actually be found, and the cities were destroyed).

Aaron became the chief spokesperson to Pharaoh instead of Moses, although Moses was God's first choice (Exodus 4:13-16).

King Hezekiah was deathly ill. The prophet announced that Hezekiah would not recover from this sickness but would die. Instead, because of his prayer, Hezekiah was granted fifteen more years of life (2 Kings 20:1, 6).

God held a brainstorming session in heaven about which strategy would be most effective in motivating King Ahab to go to war. Among the ideas that were presented, finally one was approved by God (1 Kings 22:19-22).

Ananias and Sapphira had the option either to sell their property or not to sell it, the option to keep the proceeds of the sale or to make a donation for the needs of the Jerusalem church—all these options were pleasing to God, as Peter explains it. But their lie did not please God (Acts 5:4).

In light of these various cases in dealing with God from Scripture, we learn that there is usually plenty of room within God's plan for a range of options to be pleasing to God, all of which could be considered to be within God's will. It definitely is *not* the case that there is always only *one* best means for God to accomplish his ends. We can be genuinely within God's good will to make a choice among any options that are pleasing to God

One further item needs to be clarified. In chapter four, we noted that Jesus lived in his humanity, dependent on the Father and empowered by the Holy Spirit. Jesus didn't go at life's challenges all alone. From his very early years, Jesus learned to listen to the Holy Spirit, to be tutored by the Holy Spirit to live in ways that were pleasing to God—he was led by the Holy Spirit (Luke 4:1, 14; Acts 10:38). John's Gospel, which emphasizes the role of the Father, records that Jesus did nothing of his own initiative, but did only what he saw the Father doing (John 5:19). It doesn't mean Jesus never made his own decisions. It means that Jesus continually lived in a sphere of God-confidence, always open to divine guidance in the decisions of each day.

Accordingly, Henry Blackaby and Claude King advise us, "When you see the Father at work around you, that is your invitation to adjust your life to Him and join Him in that work."[11] One means of guidance is discerning what God has already begun to do and moving in that divine flow. Yet we shouldn't limit our activity and prayer only to areas in which *we can currently detect God working.* We may be clueless about much of what God is doing and not yet have the spiritual sensitivity to perceive it. Jesus, living in complete trust in God, had gained a clear sense whenever the Father was working around him. (Our discussion in chapter three offered some points on discerning God's movements in our lives.) But we can *also* venture out beyond the evidences of God's apparent working, moving into new arenas for which God may be nudging us to move forward. In some cases, a prayer that God would answer was never asked (James 4:2)! Take the initiative, step out and see what God will do. When we step out energized by God, we restrict Satan's kingdom activity and expand the reach of God's kingdom.

Decision Making and God-Confidence

We face a number of options, opportunities and dilemmas. How do we decide what to do? Human living is much about making decisions. How do we spend our money? Should we buy this or that, or postpone buying till another time, or not buy it at all? How do we spend our time? Should we do this, or that, or do nothing at all? Or we've just been diagnosed with a physical malady. How do we proceed? Search the Web to find out more about the illness? Visit two different physicians and get a second opinion? Seek out the healing prayer-ministry team at church for some sessions of prayer? Or perhaps you're wondering which kind of living arrangement would be best for you at this season of life: sharing a room with another or having your own room? Renting an apartment or a house, or buying a house? Life is filled with choices and challenges. How do we decide what to do?

One of God's goals for us is that we become adults, wise in our decision making. The Bible makes a contrast between the wise person and the foolish person. The book of Proverbs labels those as "fools" who trust only in themselves, relying on their own perspectives when making important decisions. "Those who trust in themselves are fools, / but those who walk in wisdom are kept safe" (Proverbs 28:26 TNIV). We can all look back to difficulties and disasters we brought on ourselves because we did "our own thing" either without asking for advice or ignoring good counsel that was given. In these situations we've played the fool and suffered the consequences. But the wise learn from their mistakes, wishing to avoid that dead end again.

Listening to advice is a key virtue of the wise: "The way of fools seems right to them, / but the wise listen to advice" (Proverbs 12:15 TNIV). Since we're not all-knowing and all-wise, we seek God's guidance. Often God's guidance comes in the form of wise counsel from others. And that's part of the challenge in our faith journey: trusting someone else. Our own character faults (e.g., impatience, impulsiveness, selfishness, stubbornness, self-sufficiency and pride) can prevent us from moving ahead in trust, preventing our growth in wise decision making and in wisdom. Can we trust in this person and his or her counsel? Can we trust in God that God's principle for this situation is wisest?

And that's why we wish to explore personal guidance as one key avenue for developing greater God-confidence. In the following pages, we'll survey how God offers guidance in new ways that may stretch us beyond our comfort zones. Relying more and more on God's ways than on our own is what our journey into wisdom is all about. "Trust in the LORD with all your heart / and lean not on your own understanding; / in all your ways acknowledge him, / and he will make your paths straight" (Proverbs 3:5-6). Old Testament scholars Edward Curtis and John Brugaletta explain,

> Living wisely means receiving power from God to live and act as he designed us to live and act. He does not always tell us what choices to make. That is why He gave us the power to reason; He wants us to make some of the decisions. But He wants us to make them with Him at the center of our decision-making faculty, and thus according to His will and truth. That is what is meant by deciding wisely.[12]

Proverbs 1:7 states, "The fear of the LORD is the beginning of knowledge, / but fools despise wisdom and discipline."

God and Personal Guidance

Being finite, we all have limited perspectives, and so we desperately need wisdom for the various decisions, great and small, we must make in our life journey. Our infinite and all-wise God is in the guidance business.

> I will instruct you and teach you in the way you should go;
> I will counsel you and watch over you.
> Do not be like the horse or the mule,
> which have no understanding
> but must be controlled by bit and bridle
> or they will not come to you. (Psalm 32:8)

Do not conform any longer to the pattern of this world, but be transformed by the renewing of your mind. Then you will be able to test and approve what God's will is—his good, pleasing and perfect [moral] will. (Romans 12:2)

No temptation has seized you except what is common to man. And God is faithful; he will not let you be tempted beyond what you can bear. But when you are tempted, he will also provide a way out so that you can stand up under it. (1 Corinthians 10:13)

If any of you lacks wisdom, he should ask God, who gives generously to all without finding fault, and it will be given to him. (James 1:5)

God is more interested in helping us than we think. Unfortunately, since we usually can't see God physically nearby, we may assume he's distant, off working somewhere else, preoccupied with only the urgent and major problems of the world, with little time to give to you or me. Our view of God must change. God is so great and so grand, he's the ultimate multitasker, but without ever being hassled or abrupt or harsh. God invites each of his children to come, expectantly, and ask.

Which of you, if his son asks for bread, will give him a stone? Or if he asks for a fish, will give him a snake? If you, then, though you are evil, know how to give good gifts to your children, how much more will your Father in heaven give good gifts to those who ask him! (Matthew 7:9-11)

Additionally, one of the distinctive features of being a Christian is that God himself has taken up residence within us! The new covenant promise foretold in the Old Testament has come to pass—God the Holy Spirit now indwells each believer forever.

I will give you a new heart and put a new spirit in you; I will remove from you your heart of stone and give you a heart of flesh. And I will put my Spirit in you and move you to follow my decrees and be careful to keep my laws. (Ezekiel 36:26-27)

And I will ask the Father, and he will give you another Counselor to be with you *forever*—the Spirit of truth. (John 14:16-17, emphasis added)

The central dynamic of the Christian life is that God the Holy Spirit is in the process of sanctifying us, doing a radical character and lifestyle makeover, aiding us in putting on our "new self, created to be like God in true righteousness and holiness" (Ephesians 4:24; see also Titus 3:5-7; 1 Peter 1:2).

So then, brethren, we are under obligation, not to the flesh, to live according to the flesh—for if you are living according to the flesh, you must die; but if by the Spirit you are putting to death the deeds of the body, you will live. For all who are being led by the Spirit of God, these are sons of God. For you have not received a spirit of slavery leading to fear again, but you have received a spirit of adoption as sons by which we cry out, "Abba! Father!" The Spirit Himself testifies with our spirit that we are children of God. (Romans 8:12-16 NASB)

The Holy Spirit is not just some force or power, but is a Person of power, who mentors and coaches us and makes it possible for us to live by faith and grow into Christlikeness. Yet, in some evangelical traditions, believers are not encouraged either to talk to God the Spirit or to listen to the Spirit; only talk about God the Father or God the Son is permitted. Yet the Holy Spirit is the agent of the trinitarian Godhead for our sanctification (e.g., John 16:7, 13-16; 2 Thessalonians 2:13; 1 Peter 1:2).

Furthermore, although we are always indwelt by the Spirit, we also need constantly to be "filled by the Spirit," to intentionally co-ordinate our decision making and life walk with the Spirit. That's how Jesus lived his life here. As was presented in chapter four, Jesus depended on the Holy Spirit during his thirty-plus years on this earth, living in the power of the Spirit, showing us how it's done, leaving us an example to follow. The only way we can live the kind of life that pleases God is by "keep[ing] in step with the Spirit" (Galatians 5:25). This is an important relational dynamic—we are never alone. God himself is always near, and within, us.

In the sections that follow, we highlight those means of guidance particularly related to aspects of our inner life. We're not intending to dismiss or devalue cognitive factors—both of us are commit-ted to the life of the mind, and we both teach graduate students at Talbot School of Theology at Biola University. As a part of seeking guidance, we strongly encourage gaining more information by at-tending conferences and reading what experts and mature Chris-tians have to say about matters for which we seek guidance. We're glad you're reading this book! Perhaps you'll want to read some of the resources we've listed in each chapter in the endnotes. From this point on, we'll explore how God's Spirit can guide us—through God's Word that is Spirit-inspired, through help from within the Christian community as the Spirit leads them to offer counsel to us, and through the witness of the Spirit within, including particular avenues for guidance that don't usually get sufficient attention.

Guidance through study of and meditation on God's Word. God has revealed himself uniquely in his Word. The Bible is fairly clear that God has an opinion about what kind of lifestyle is best for us. The study and meditation of God's Word is the preeminent source of divine guidance. Psalm 1 promises a life of success that pleases God for those who regularly meditate on God's Word. Psalm 19:7-14 is more specific:

The law of the LORD is perfect,
   reviving the soul.
The statutes of the LORD are trustworthy,
   making wise the simple.
The precepts of the LORD are right,
   giving joy to the heart.
The commands of the LORD are radiant,
   giving light to the eyes.
The fear of the LORD is pure,
   enduring forever.
The ordinances of the LORD are sure
   and altogether righteous.
They are more precious than gold,
   than much pure gold;
they are sweeter than honey,
   than honey from the comb.
By them is your servant warned;
   in keeping them there is great reward.

Who can discern his errors?
   Forgive my hidden faults.
Keep your servant also from willful sins;
   may they not rule over me.
Then will I be blameless,
   innocent of great transgression.

May the words of my mouth and the meditation of my heart

be pleasing in your sight,

O LORD, my Rock and my Redeemer.

God's Word affects our lives in many ways: "reviving the soul," "giving joy to the heart," "giving light to the eyes," warning us away from sin and offering great reward—a life that is successful in God's eyes.

One morning while I (Klaus) was on an extended spiritual retreat God powerfully intervened through his Word like never before in my life. The spiritual mentor supervising this retreat sensed God was stirring something in me and encouraged me to seek God diligently—although I was clueless about those stirrings. And so I earnestly asked God to help me see more clearly what he was doing. I fasted for the first time I can remember. The weekend passed without any direction or insights. A bit frustrated, I continued seeking nonetheless. Monday morning began as usual, with only liquids for breakfast to maintain the fast. I asked the Lord what I should do, and the word *Romans* came to mind. So, I knelt at my bed and began reading Romans 1. But when I got to verses 30 and 31, these words jumped out at me: "arrogant," "boastful," "unloving," "unmerciful." They became living and active words of conviction, prying open my heart, uncovering a layer of sinfulness hidden from me, a layer of pride I could not sense.

God was tenderly yet forcefully making me aware of my sinfulness in the presence of his own holiness. Since coming to Christ at a young age, I had never genuinely sensed my sin. But at this moment (in my mid forties at the time), God visited me in this vivid and life-changing divine encounter. While I continued reading Romans, the words persistently penetrated my heart with such force that for two hours I cried in the presence of God. God loved me enough to make me aware, at a deep experiential level, of my own pride and sinfulness, and my desperate need for his mercy and continuing work in my life as a believer. Although having served God as a pastor, and now a seminary professor, I was not exempt from this vile sin of pride. Some have blocked arteries; I had clogged spiritual veins. The cholesterol of self-righteousness minimized (and still minimizes) the work God could do through me.

During my college years, I had spent more time meditating on God's Word, but since my seminary days, I tended to approach Scripture more intellectually, with my mind only. Peter Toon identifies this problem: "The separation of the *scholarly* pursuit from the *devotional* use of the Bible is not inevitable, but it is common."[13] Now I've come to appreciate the importance of also *meditating* on Bible passages. But note that these approaches to Scripture, study and meditation are complementary, not competing. "Once your mind is full of the text, its *meaning,* and some possible applications, take time to reflect on it *prayerfully.* . . . Let there be a time for you yourself to respond to the Word of God."[14]

The *analytical* mode for the reading and study of Scripture is highly honored in the scholarly evangelical tradition. The words *Bible study, exegesis* and *hermeneutics* are associated with this approach in which we bring questions to the text and analyze it in order to gain knowledge of the truth. Analytical reading highlights the use of our God-given minds to master the public meaning of the God-given written text, an essential process to discern the objective truth of God's special revelation. We wrestle with the written Word to winnow out the author's intended meaning resident in the text in order to know the truth. We are on a mission, and we ply the text with questions until we discern the answers.

Yet *meditative* Scripture reading also offers a rich opportunity to visit with God, although it has not been discussed much in our particular evangelical tradition. Evangelicals have begun to recognize the need for both approaches, yet the question is, how do these approaches relate to each other? Our preference is to engage them in a *cyclical* process, now employing an analytical mode, now pausing to engage the meditative mode, then again employing an analytical mode, and pausing again to engage the meditative mode and so on. Through such repetitive movement we can seek understanding of truth and universal principles for living and welcome God's penetrating and personal touch on our lives.[15]

Meditative reading is of a different tone and texture and adds another dimension to how the Bible can affect our lives. Here we patiently wait and listen for God to speak to us personally. Our purpose is not to master a certain portion of Scripture, but to read a few verses, slowly, meditatively, perhaps vocalizing each word, and monitoring our heart to sense God's movement to highlight a certain word or phrase or sentence for our attentive reflection and rumination. In meditative reading, we have no agenda; there is no hurry to read so many verses, to pose questions of the text, no need to control or direct our reading. We wish to be ready for God to speak to us personally. With David we invite God to expose the depth of our soul: "Search me, O God, and know my heart; / test me and know my anxious thoughts. / See if there is any offensive way in me, / and lead me in the way everlasting" (Psalm 139:23-24). And with the child Samuel we open ourselves to God with submission, "Speak, for your servant is listening" (1 Samuel 3:10).

If the one mode could be categorized as exploring and researching, the other might best be viewed as listening and hearing. These two modes—analytical and meditative Scripture reading—involve, I believe, a symbiotic relationship and are so distinctly different that they may seem almost mutually exclusive. That is, it is difficult to practice both simultaneously—at least it is so for me—if I desire to be true to the dictates of each format. Rather, we engage in them sequentially, one at a time, yet not in a linear fashion of first step being completed by the second step.

So the overall process of analysis and meditation probably works better as a sequential process, perhaps more like a continuous and repetitive cycle, like that of a spinning wheel. We need both analytical and meditative approaches to Scripture if we wish to be fully responsive to God's transforming work in our lives through his Word.

Both a *textual* focus and a *relational/personal* focus are necessary in our engagement with the Scriptures. Notice the connection between Hebrews 4:12 and 4:13:

> For the word of God is living and active. Sharper than any double-edged sword, it penetrates even to dividing soul and spirit, joints and marrow; it judges the thoughts and attitudes of the heart. (Hebrews 4:12)

> Nothing in all creation is hidden from God's sight. Everything is uncovered and laid bare before the eyes of him to whom we must give account. (Hebrews 4:13)

William Lane explains, "In context, the force of v 13 is to assert that exposure to the word of Scripture entails exposure to God himself."[16] Similarly, Gerhard Maier says,

> The Bible is far more than a treasure trove of doctrinal truths. To view it [only] as a catalog of God's utterances would be to mistake its character. It is primarily communication of God—communication in the literal sense: God himself communes with us. He wants us to experience communion with him.[17]

In the meditative approach to Scripture, we place ourselves in a context of openness to the mystery of God, with no real agenda, as he seeks to touch our lives in the deep places. For, if we wish to seek a personal word from God, nowhere else can we be as certain of hearing God's voice as when we are listening to the very words of God in Scripture. This opportunity is possible because the Bible is the Word *of God,* not a Word detached from God. We come to Scripture as a conversation *with* God. For myself, I've found it helpful to stop asking questions when I enter a meditative mode. Otherwise my trained exegetical mind will keep up an onslaught of questions, which often place a distance between the text and God and me. I purposely shut off the questioning to be in a posture of receptivity, whatever God wishes to show me.

As I engage in meditative Scripture reading, although I am expectant, I am always *surprised* when a thought comes out of the blue, redirecting my focus from where it was to a new place of thought or feeling, toward a certain word, phrase or concept that God wanted me to ponder. Consider a few personal examples from a time I was meditating on the life of Jesus in the Gospels. From the story of the four who lowered their friend through a roof for Jesus to heal him (Mark 2), I was prompted to consider, Am I one who prays for my friends to that degree? As I read Mark 2:20 ("But the time will come when the bridegroom will be taken away from them, and on that day they will fast"), for the first time from that passage I experienced a deep sadness that, of course, Jesus knew so early in his ministry that he would face death in the near future.

Surely our analytical reading and study of Scripture sets an important context to engage in meditative, prayerful reading of Scripture. Any personal touch of God will have some connection to the public meaning of the text, as Michael Casey notes,

> In one sense there is not much point in spending time with the Scriptures if we are not diligent in searching out the authentic meaning of the text before us. . . . It is true that there are passages in the Scriptures that speak to us with urgency and passion even without preparation on our part. It is also true that we often fumble and miss the meaning of a text simply because we have not taken the trouble to do the necessary spade work.[18]

Our increasing knowledge of Scripture provides an important informational framework for meditative reading. After slowly reading the passage, I usually consult a good commentary or reference work to help me become aware of factors that may contribute to my deeper appreciation of the passage. With this informational context, I can proceed with my meditation of the passage and perceive the personal significance of the text for me.

Inviting others to help us seek divine guidance. Along with recognizing that Scripture has a central role in providing guidance, we also want to note the importance of Christian community, and seeking the counsel of mature Christians who are led by the Spirit themselves (Galatians 5:16). Sadly, our Western culture is radically individualistic; we're encouraged to give more effort and priority to tasks and busyness than to relationships. Relationships are just a means to getting things done. But a healthy biblical view accepts the value of both individual and community; neither can be neglected. Each of us will be individually accountable to Jesus Christ for how we lived our life on earth (2 Corinthians 5:10). But being connected within a Christian community is a strong biblical theme (e.g., Ephesians 4:1-16). It's important for each believer to grow in trust and intimacy with brothers and sisters in Christ, spending time to cultivate deeper relationships.[19]

I greatly appreciated the help J. P. offered me a while back regarding a financial quagmire. But I had to be open to admitting to him my foolishness. I was embarrassed to reveal my poor financial health, but it was well worth it. With some hard decisions, good planning and discipline over a two-year period, I was able to move into a healthier financial position. J. P. and I have benefited from guidance received from wise counselors in spiritual direction and Christian therapy. "Walk with the wise and become wise," Proverbs 13:20 says (NIV). Richard Foster encourages believers facing important decisions to invite others to help discern the Lord's leading for that person ("corporate guidance"), whether it be launching into a new life direction, starting a new organization or even considering marriage.[20]

As a part of being connected to the body of Christ, we have also appreciated new avenues in which fellow believers have ministered to us. It's been such a rich experience for both of us to receive prayer by a team of people. So we've now taken similar training at our church and participate ourselves on teams to pray for others. One memorable time of being prayed for occurred while I (Klaus) attended a conference at another church a couple of years ago. An announcement was made that we could sign up to be prayed over by a team of four people for about fifteen minutes. As I showed up for my prayer appointment and sat down, one person began to pray by affirming my teaching ministry; another stated that I liked to solve "Bible problems" and that I shouldn't rely on my own resources since God would provide the answers. And they continued to pray like that. None of the people knew me from Adam, yet their words fit me to a tee. I began to weep, being deeply touched, realizing God was speaking to me. Of course, often in prayer times, those who pray are voicing their own ideas and perspectives. Yet in some cases, God works through words being offered to convey his own message to us, which can strike very deeply as it did me that day.[21]

Here we must note Matthew 18:20: "For where two or three come together in my name, *there am I with them*" (emphasis added). The particular context for Jesus' promise appears within the practice of church reconciliation for a sinning brother or sister; "two or three" relates to the legal number of witnesses in the Old Testament (e.g., Deuteronomy 19:15). Yet there is a deeper principle and promise underlying this verse that goes beyond these particular circumstances. Each believer now lives "in Christ" (Colossians 1:27; John 15:1-5), each being indwelt forever (John 14:16) by the Holy Spirit, who conveys the presence of God to us (i.e., fellowship with God created by the Spirit, 2 Corinthians 13:14). Since a deep relational unity

among believers is one of God's important goals—as indicated in
Jesus' prayer to the Father "that they may be one as we are one" (John
17:11, 22)—whenever believers gather together, especially in a har-
mony of will about a matter, the Holy Spirit, the one who is the very
"Spirit of Christ" (Romans 8:9; 1 Peter 1:11), is present sustaining
this unity (Ephesians 4:3; Philippians 2:1-2).

The Spirit can guide through inner words. In addition to Scripture study and meditation and the counsel of others, the Holy Spirit
may also guide us personally from within (the inner witness of the
Spirit, Romans 8:16), if we're alert and ready. God promises, "I will
instruct you and teach you in the way you should go; / I will counsel
you and watch over you" (Psalm 32:8).

The Spirit can prompt words or ideas as we're thinking (e.g., Luke
12:11-12; Acts 8:39; 13:12). The Spirit can also give us images or
pictures to ponder rather than just words. The Spirit can also work
in our feelings and desires (e.g., Matthew 20:32-34; Luke 22:59-62;
John 16:8; 2 Corinthians 1:3-4; Galatians 5:22-23; Philippians
4:6-7), as was discussed in chapter three. As one Old Testament
scholar reminds us, "One way I know God's will is by the desires
of my heart. . . . When God is in control of your life, He is also in
control of your desires. The things you long for in your heart are put
there by the Holy Spirit."[22] Attending to these inner avenues of divine guidance has not always been emphasized within our particular
tradition. Perhaps we've become persuaded that Satan can easily use
these particular avenues to tempt us away from God. But cannot
God use them for good as he did in Bible times? Satan can only copy
and distort. Why do we tend to ascribe to Satan more power than we
attribute to God? Of course, we must be aware that Satan will try to
distract us, yet we don't want to limit how God can get his message
through to us.

Have you ever experienced a word or an idea that popped into
your head that led to good results? God can be the source of this,

something Nehemiah experienced: "I set out during the night with a few men. I had not told anyone *what my God had put in my heart* to do for Jerusalem" (Nehemiah 2:12, emphasis added; see also Luke 12:11-12; Acts 8:39; 13:12). In his book *Does God Still Guide?* British preacher J. Sidlow Baxter shares how a pastor friend of his was led to take a train ride to visit someone whom he had never met. While in his office "his mind was suddenly gripped by a strong conviction that he should visit a certain jail, to see a man who was under death sentence for murder."[23] He knew the circumstances of the crime, but it was a long journey away and, besides, he had much to do in the pastorate. "Yet he had been praying, earlier, that the day might be guided, and he was convinced now that the strange urge was from the Holy Spirit." Despite delays and almost missing connections, he arrived at the prison, but then had to wait for official permission.

Finally, face to face with the prisoner through a small grating in the cell door, he explained the unusual circumstances for being there despite the various delays. At that moment in the background the prison clock boomed twice, announcing two o'clock. Immediately the prisoner "burst into convulsing sobbing." Through his tears and sobbing, he confessed, "I never meant to kill . . . but . . . I am to die . . . This morning, in my agony, I cried, 'Oh God, if you really exist, and if you really hear, and if you care, please, oh please, let me know in *some way* . . . and, oh, God, I give you until two o'clock this afternoon.'" The pastor left some time later having witnessed the prisoner's response to Jesus' invitation for eternal life, and possessing a sense of gratefulness that he himself had responded to God's guidance earlier that day.

A student of mine, Martha, had completed all the requirements for her real estate license, but still needed to complete the final California state registration process. She had tried the Internet registration site, but couldn't figure out how to do it. Phoning the state office in Sacramento was problematic. She was left on hold for what seemed like hours and never talked to anyone before the office closed at five o'clock. Or, when she remembered to make the call, it was already after hours. One late afternoon while at home, she "heard" these words in her mind, "Call the real estate office." It was 4:30 p.m. Martha quickly dialed the number and was placed on hold. She prayed that someone would answer the phone within the next twenty-five minutes, since she had past experiences of being on hold for up to an hour and the office always closed at five o'clock. At 4:55 p.m., a state employee answered her call and kindly talked her through the online registration process. He also reminded her that she had only five more days to complete the registration; otherwise she'd have to start all over, since the one-year window of opportunity was coming to a close. Martha got the required forms in and received her license. She praised God for reminding her to make the call and for having someone answer before five o'clock.

The Spirit used an interesting way to encourage Halee, a colleague at another Christian college in California, and her husband, Paul, to pack up their bags and move to California from Texas, her home state. In August 2001, Paul and Halee had just returned from their honeymoon in California. They had only been married a month and were excited about starting their new lives together in their new home in Plano, Texas (a suburb of Dallas). One day Halee was in her favorite bookstore with a friend, and Halee became aware that every book she laid her eyes on had the word *California* in the title. She sensed that this was more than a coincidence, that God was saying something. A bit disturbed, Halee fled to a section of the store she felt would be free of any geographical references. But the book titled *California Cooking* caught her eye. As she stared at these words, the Lord spoke to her, "Halee, you're moving to California."

That evening was Paul and Halee's weekly "date night." Since she knew Paul never wanted to go back to California where he had been raised, Halee decided to hold off sharing her bookstore experience till later in the evening. She wanted to see whether God would speak to Paul about the matter as well. They ordered their food at the restaurant. Paul fiddled with his food. Halee asked him if something was on his mind, and Paul responded, "I'm not sure what to make of this, but I was sitting at work today, and I was overwhelmed by the idea that we're going to move to California. But I don't know—it may mean nothing." Halee looked at Paul and said, "Oh, well I know we are," and shared what happened in the bookstore.

Halee knew they would be moving at some point, but for months she struggled with the idea of leaving Texas—all her life had been there, and she would be leaving behind her extended family. She wrestled with her own feelings and the grief her extended family would experience. During her quiet time one morning, while working through Genesis, Genesis 12:1 jumped out at her: "The LORD had said to Abram, 'Leave your country, your people and your father's household and go to the land I will show you.'" Halee wondered how difficult it must have been for Abram and Sarai to leave all that was familiar to them and go to a place they had never been before. In one sense, theirs was a greater move than the one she and Paul were anticipating. Halee was comforted by this passage and strengthened to do what God had asked her to do. In this case, God talked to Paul and Halee the same day about the move, then months later confirmed the message through a scriptural passage to address Halee's concerns about the move.

"This child will bring joy to the world." These were the words spoken to a single mother in a time of great turmoil. Myra was contemplating an abortion, for the child she carried was the result of rape. She responded to these words of hope, and many years later this child, James Robison, born in 1943, became an evangelist whom God would use to bring many to himself.[24]

Dr. John Finch, a former spiritual mentor of mine, was about to commit suicide by jumping over the rails of a cruise ship sailing between Australia and Antarctica one stormy dark night. In his late sixties, he had lost his professional psychology license due to a professional and moral indiscretion. While on the cruise ship, he fell into a deep depression and wanted to end his life. As he began to climb the rails to jump overboard, above the roar of the storm and sea John heard a loving voice say, "But I love you." These words touched him deeply because, as a young child, his British parents in India had dropped him off at a boarding school, and never returned to pick him up. John refocused his ministry toward leading extended three-week spiritual retreats.[25] Both Beth and I (Klaus) benefited from this ministry.

Sometimes God may even use our own words to give us his perspective on the matter. Jayne Thurber-Smith had contributed a few short pieces of writing to a daily devotional series. As it turned out, it was four years before the book was published in 2003 and Jayne read one of her devotionals, dated September 7, "Give thanks in all circumstances." The original piece had been written in March 1999 during a time when her husband was between jobs. Finances were tight, and God had ministered to Jayne through 1 Thessalonians 5:18: "Give thanks in all circumstances, for this is God's will for you in Christ Jesus." Three years later, in March 2002, her brother Troy died of lymphona, and Jayne had a difficult time with his death and was very angry that God hadn't healed him. Those were difficult times, especially on September 7, Troy's birthday. The next year in August, copies of her devotionals arrived in the mail, just a month before the anniversary of her brother's death. When she read the devotional that had been assigned to September 7 in her book, "God spoke to me through the words of a younger Jayne. . . . I learned . . . to be thankful for the time I had with Troy instead of complaining that he had to go home to heaven."[26]

Sometimes God's initial guidance is difficult to figure out, even ambiguous at times. Perhaps God's purpose in such perplexing situations is to see whether we're willing to follow the initial light to seek more. While Moses was on the back side of the desert tending sheep, he happened to notice a burning bush. Instead of ignoring it, he was curious to find out more and walked closer to it; only then did God speak to Moses (Exodus 3:1-5).

While hungry and waiting for lunch to be prepared, the apostle Peter was praying on a rooftop. He fell into a trance and saw descending a sheet that was full of clean and unclean animals, and he heard a voice that urged, "Get up, Peter. Kill and eat!" (Acts 10:9-13). Three times this happened; each time when Peter declined, the voice said, "Do not call anything impure that God has made clean" (Acts 10:14-16). Then Luke records, "While Peter was *wondering about the meaning of the vision,* the men sent by Cornelius found out where Simon's house was and stopped at the gate" (Acts 10:17, emphasis added). Over the next day it became clear to Peter that, first, no ethnic group is unclean to God (Acts 10:28) and, furthermore, that God also saves non-Jews (Acts 10:34-35). God confirmed these insights for Peter by sending the Holy Spirit upon all the Gentiles in Cornelius's house, an event called the Gentile Pentecost.

On a grander scale, clear teaching of the doctrine of the Trinity had to wait, in the progress of revelation, until Jesus Christ's teaching during New Testament times. Only now looking back with New Testament eyes can we see evidence for a Trinity in the Old Testament. Therefore, at the practical level, although God promises to provide personal guidance (Psalm 32:8-9; James 1:5), we may not discern the meaning of initial divine guidance, so we'll need to persist in asking God to get the full message.

Of course Satan will also suggest ideas in our thinking, so we'll need to monitor our self-talk, the thoughts that regularly pass through our minds (see 2 Corinthians 10:5; Philippians 4:8). God will *only* speak loving truth that liberates; Satan will only speak ensnaring *lies* and *half-truths* that imprison and lead to destruction. Jesus alerts us to Satan's deceptive strategy, "When [the devil] lies, he speaks his native language, for he is a liar and the father of lies" (John 8:44). Any negative or disparaging self-talk is never from God, but is from the pit of hell, for as Jesus clarifies, "The thief [i.e., Satan] comes only to steal and kill and destroy; I have come that they may have life, and have it to the full" (John 10:10). As God's children, we can learn how to listen for God's loving words of truth that will always pierce and shatter the falsehoods and evil traps of Satan.

The Spirit can guide through images or pictures within. Not only can God give us thoughts to guide us, but he can also provide images or pictures. In chapter three we included the account of how Jesus ministered to my (Klaus's) wife, Beth, through a vivid image of an ice-skating scene in which Jesus stood behind her by a warm fire, to assure her of his presence at a time when she felt alone. For pastor Ray Pritchard, God used a dramatic picture to redirect the church's ministry. A number of issues came to a head, leading Calvary Church in Oak Park (a suburb of Chicago) into a time of crisis. One man even told Pastor Ray he should never be in the pastorate and that he would work to see that Pastor Ray would never be a pastor again! Shortly thereafter, it happened that Pastor Ray was scheduled to be on a teaching mission in Belize.

> There in the jungle, far removed from all the controversy, I had a powerful experience of the Holy Spirit. I pictured the church with a large black cloud hanging over it. It seemed that the Lord was saying to me, "You have seen what you can do, but you have no answers for this problem." I came to a deep conviction that the cloud would not lift by preaching or programs but only by prayer. When I shared that with the congregation upon my return, the people were deeply moved. Out of that came the prayer movement at Calvary, and I look back on that as the turning point of my entire ministry in Oak Park.[27]

For one of my Biola colleagues, God used a dream as a key turning point in helping him move from a more moralistic and performance-oriented view of the Christian life toward a more grace-oriented one. While in college, someone

> tried to explain to me the nature, reality, and totality of God's grace. I wrestled with this for the next few years, and "argued" with God about it. For someone weaned on the belief that my own effort was a key part of my salvation, accepting that God's grace is a free gift of His love, and that all my works didn't count one whit to pay for His immense salvation, was a radical and exceedingly difficult change for my mind and heart.

Then early one morning, he had a dream in which a robed person—an angel he thought—walked past his bed from left to right, speaking in a loud voice, "Romans 8:2 and 2:28, Romans 8:2 and 2:28!" Then the angel disappeared, and my colleague awoke suddenly. Immediately he got out his Bible and read,

> Because through Christ Jesus the law of the Spirit of life set me free from the law of sin and death. (Romans 8:2)

> A man is not a Jew if he is only one outwardly, nor is circumcision merely outward and physical. No, a man is a Jew if he is one inwardly; and circumcision is circumcision of the heart, by the Spirit, not by the written code. Such a man's praise is not from men, but from God. (Romans 2:28-29)

He wrote to me,

> The truth of God's Word pierced my heart. My outward efforts could not merit any percentage of God's favor at all. God's grace is immense and free. All my life I have been humbled that the life-giving Spirit chose such a potent, compelling way to speak to a struggling child.[28]

What about dreams? What do we make of dreams and divine guidance? In our view, most dreams are related to matters of our inner life, conveyed in symbolic form—the people and places in our dreams usually depict inner states within ourselves—providing a way for the deep things in our souls to touch us through vivid imagery and feelings rather than through abstract concepts. Although everyone dreams, many of us do not remember most of our dreams. I (Klaus) am one who infrequently remembers a dream. One dream that had a profound effect on me involved the unusual circumstances of driving to a parking lot to catch a bus to go to a Christian-themed amusement park—a bizarre scenario to my mind now. In the dream, when we arrived at the parking lot, Beth and I got out of the car. We then were supposed to go to a shuttle that would take us to the amusement park. Beth had her bag lunch with her, but I had to go to another area to find mine—which proved very frustrating. I finally found my lunch, but then the shuttle with Beth in it had already left. And that was the tenor of the dream, always being late.

But all these details were secondary to my particular actions and the feelings I experienced in the dream. The takeaway message had three major points: always trying to catch up, always in a rush and separated from Beth. It was another wake-up call that my workaholism continued to drive my life. I never had time for much solitude, and my busyness prevented me from spending more time with Beth. This dream was one means among others God used to help me face my problem and begin taking steps to be less busy.[29]

Yet we always believe that some dreams come from God, as the Bible teaches. You can't get through Matthew's telling of the Christmas story without encountering several dreams of divine guidance, either given to Joseph (to become married to Mary, Matthew 1:20-24; to leave Bethlehem for Egypt before Herod's slaughter of the babies, Matthew 2:13-14; to return from Egypt to Israel, Matthew 2:19-20; and to avoid living in Judea, Matthew 2:22) or to the Magi who came to worship the child Jesus (Matthew 2:12). During Old Testament times, God spoke through dreams to believers (e.g., Jacob, Genesis 28:12; Joseph, Genesis 37:5; Solomon, 1 Kings 3:5-15; Daniel, Daniel 7:1) and unbelievers alike (e.g., Abimelech, Genesis 20:3-6; Pharaoh, Genesis 41:1-8; a Midianite soldier, Judges 7:13-15; Nebuchadnezzar, Daniel 2:1). In one interesting situation, God assured Gideon of victory over the Midianites by having Gideon overhear one Midianite soldier share a dream with his colleague. The colleague interpreted the dream.

> His friend responded, "This can be nothing other than the sword of Gideon son of Joash, the Israelite. God has given the Midianites and the whole camp into his hands."
>
> When Gideon heard the dream and its interpretation, he worshiped God. He returned to the camp of Israel and called out, "Get up! The LORD has given the Midianite camp into your hands." (Judges 7:14-15)

Of course, Satan has the power to give deceptive dreams to lead people away from God (Deuteronomy 13:1-5; Jeremiah 23:25; Zechariah 10:2; Jude 8), to torment people with fearful nightmares (perhaps Psalm 73:19-20 is an allusion to a nightmare) and to make visions appear (e.g., some scholars explain that during the temptation, Jesus was given a vision of all the kingdoms of the world, Luke 4:5; 2 Corinthians 11:14).

Dreams in the early church. Although the early church welcomed dreams as one means for God to speak to them, there is good evidence to indicate that dreams were brought into disrepute in the church by a mistranslation in the Vulgate, the Latin translation of the Bible that became the standard version for the church for a thousand years. Jerome, the translator of the Vulgate, was himself significantly influenced toward more biblical studies by a stunning dream. During an illness, probably during his desert stay in A.D.

376, Jerome dreamed that he was dragged before a judge who asked him to establish his religious identity (as was done before believers were martyred). Jerome replied that he was a Christian, to which the judge responded, "You are a follower of Cicero, not of Christ," signifying that Jerome devoted more attention to the classical pagan literature than to Scripture. While being scourged, Jerome pleaded for mercy, and then made an oath that he would forsake "worldly books." He awoke from the dream drenched in tears and under conviction. "Thencefore I read the books of God with a zeal greater than I had previously given to the books of men."[30] The dream became a turning point regarding the focus of his study. Eventually Jerome devoted his life to the study of Scripture, including the Latin translation of the Bible.

As Morton Kelsey explains, despite God using such a vivid dream in Jerome's own life, for some unknown reason, in his translation of the Old Testament, Jerome associated "observing dreams" with the practice of sorcery in three particular Old Testament verses (Leviticus 19:26; Deuteronomy 18:10; 2 Chronicles 33:6; where "witchcraft" or "sorcery" appears in our English versions, the words "observing dreams" appeared).[31] Eventually dreams fell out of favor as a common means of divine guidance through much of church history. In the last century, Sigmund Freud gave attention to dreams as an important source of unconscious aspects of the inner life of a person, yet his interpretive framework of an overly sexual interpretive scheme didn't help make dreams very palatable for Christians. But Freud's original interpretive framework is no longer the mainstay in psychology. Currently, dreams are being welcomed again by various Christian leaders as legitimate means for gaining insight into our inner lives and as a way God can communicate to us.

Vivid guidance through dreams. God used an interesting sequence of events to guide an evangelical theology professor to a new place of ministry. Over the years, another seminary had regularly invited

Dr. Jones (not his real name) to join their faculty, but he didn't sense a clear leading to leave his current place of teaching. One January, he needed to give an indication to the seminary whether he would consider their invitation or not. This was a perplexing situation, and Dr. Jones continued to ask God for guidance in the matter. One evening that week, he was up late pondering the dilemma and his child, who couldn't sleep, came into his den and sat on his lap. The child asked what he was thinking about, and he explained the invitation of the seminary. The child responded with this question, "How many theologians are at your seminary?" And he gave an answer. "And how many theologians are at this other seminary?" Dr. Jones replied that there was a much smaller number. "It seems to me," the child reflected, "wouldn't God want more theologians at the other seminary?" Out of the mouths of babes?

The following Sunday, a church member stopped Dr. Jones in the hallway and said, "So, you'll be moving soon." He was shocked. Only his immediate family and the particular seminary knew of the possibility. Dr Jones asked what she meant. Although she was not given to these unusual experiences, she admitted she had had a dream the night before. As she shared the details of the dream, this theology professor—also not used to such means of divine guidance—was stunned by the relevance of the details to his situation. In the dream, Dr. Jones was carrying his briefcase, leaving his seminary office and walking out the door. Then he would return to his seminary office, open the door and enter the office. Then, again, leave his office and again return to his office. This movement back and forth went on for some time (perhaps indicating the quandary of which way to choose). Finally, Dr. Jones returned to his office, but the office door was locked and he couldn't get back in. So he left his seminary office, never to return. As the dream was being narrated, Dr. Jones's heart was being stirred. God seemed to be confirming his direction to make a move.

He then asked if in the dream there was any mention of which city he was moving to. She responded, "Yes, Philadelphia!" But that did not compute; there was no seminary in Philadelphia that had contacted him. His initial euphoria subsided, and he was back in the quandary again. Later that day, the Lord brought to mind that Philadelphia was mentioned in the Bible, in the section of Revelation concerning the seven churches. Turning to Revelation 3:7-8, he read:

> To the angel of the church in Philadelphia write:
>
> > These are the words of him who is holy and true, who holds the key of David. What he opens no one can shut, and what he shuts no one can open. I know your deeds. See, I have placed before you an open door that no one can shut.

The reference to the closed door and open door of the dream confirmed to Dr. Jones that God was directing him to move, which he then did. He's been there now serving at this seminary several years. In this case the dream was symbolic, yet in some cases dreams are so relevant that they depict actual life situations.

God used a dream to save Laura Hatch's life. The seventeen-year-old Seattle senior high student left a party late one night, October 2, 2004, but never returned home. Her parents, Todd and Jean Hatch, along with relatives and friends, searched high and low, but she was nowhere to be found. Prayer support and vast e-mail support encouraged the family to keep hoping. After many days of searching, most thought she was dead. The sheriff's deputies finally wrote her off as a runaway. But one night Sha Nohr, a fellow member at the Hatches' church, woke up suddenly from a vivid dream about where Laura was and with an urgency to look for Laura. So that morning, October 10, along with her daughter, Sha drove out to some wooded areas indicated in the dream, praying for guidance from God. They finally spotted Laura's car off a winding road, two hundred feet down in a ravine. Laura had missed a curve, and the car had tumbled down a ravine, out of sight from the road. Due to the trauma of the accident and broken bones, mostly around her face, she couldn't get out of the car. She had survived eight days without food or water! Officials called it a medical miracle. Doctors reported that her dehydration had actually prevented the expansion of a blood clot in her brain. Her mother said, "We have been prayed for by people all over the Earth, literally. In this case, in a very tangible way, their prayers and our prayers have been answered."[32]

The last two stories offer examples for how the divine guidance we seek may come through the counsel and ministry of others.

The Spirit can guide through our longings. Before we close this section on means of guidance, we must note that God also guides us through our desires, our longings, a topic treated in chapter three. As we noted in that chapter, Old Testament scholar Bruce Waltke explained that we need to listen to our desires: "One way I know God's will is by the desires of my heart. When God is in control of your life, He is also in control of your desires. The things you long for in your heart are put there by the Holy Spirit."[33] As we also pointed out in chapter three, C. S. Lewis reminded us that we tend to settle for less, when more is possible: "Indeed, if we consider the unblushing promises of reward and the staggering nature of the rewards promised in the Gospels, it would seem that *Our Lord finds our desires not too strong, but too weak. . . . We are far too easily pleased.*"[34] Old Testament scholar John Goldingay translates Psalm 37:4 this way: "Take delight in Yhwh so that he may give you the requests of your heart."[35] Goldingay explains that taking delight in God is related to our God-confidence:

> Delight in Yhwh is a more affective version of trust in Yhwh or
> a more affective version of the idea of seeking help from Yhwh

that appears elsewhere. . . . But they are indeed the requests of the heart: the listeners are invited to bring their deepest longings to Yhwh so that they can be fulfilled.[36]

King David, who penned Psalm 37:4, desired to build a temple, a permanent house for God, since worship to God had been carried out in a tabernacle-tent since the days of Moses (2 Samuel 7:1-3). Although God only permitted David to provide the building materials so Solomon could build the temple (1 Chronicles 28:1-8), God honored David's heart desire by making a commitment to build David's "house," his lineage, his kingdom, which would eventually include the Messiah as King, a promise we call the Davidic Covenant (2 Samuel 7:8-16; Psalm 89:19-37).

But the challenge for us is knowing what really *are* our deepest longings. We're not saying that any desire will please God, for sadly we often bring with us into the Christian life various "evil desires" (Romans 6:12; Colossians 3:5; 1 Peter 1:14; 2 Peter 1:4). For example, in the early church a married couple, Ananias and Sapphira, wanted to be viewed as generous just like Barnabas (Acts 4:36-37). But they kept back a portion of the sale of land, claiming to have given all as Barnabas had done. Peter accused them of lying to God (Acts 5:1-11). Like this couple, we may confuse our learned compulsions for legitimate good desires, but these are only dysfunctional substitutes, such as perfectionism, control issues, people pleasing, narcissism, selfishness, arrogance and the like. These vices are of the dark kingdom and need to be healed. James instructs us:

> But if you harbor bitter envy and selfish ambition in your hearts, do not boast about it or deny the truth. Such "wisdom" does not come down from heaven but is earthly, unspiritual, of the devil. For where you have envy and selfish ambition, there you find disorder and every evil practice.

But the wisdom that comes from heaven is first of all pure; then peace-loving, considerate, submissive, full of mercy and good fruit, impartial and sincere. (James 3:14-17)

We have been created in the image of God (Genesis 1:26) and are now being conformed to the image of his Son (Romans 8:29). We are made with deep longings for relationship, unity and friendship; for personal wholeness in ourselves and in others; and for doing good for others (e.g., Luke 22:15; John 17:24; 1 Thessalonians 3:6; Romans 10:1; 15:23; 2 Corinthians 5:2; 1 Timothy 3:1; 2 Timothy 3:12; Jude 5).

In chapter three we described how we can become much more aware of the movings of our heart, for good and for ill, and also how Satan's desire is to hijack our good desires and distract us from God's ways. Yet despite the evil in our hearts (Jeremiah 17:9), we must not ignore the biblical teaching that God also moves within us for good, in our deepest longings (Psalm 37:4). We started this chapter with the story of Ken Eldred, in whom God had placed the deep desire to serve him through a calling in business. God confirmed that longing over a period of time, as he led Ken first to clarify his primary commitment to God himself. Likewise, with God's help, we can get better at recognizing God's movement within our longings to lead us into doing what pleases him.[37]

Taking Risks: Being Receptive to God's Guidance

It may be the case that God has been offering you indicators of guidance, but you haven't noticed, being unaware of how God can speak. We hope our discussion in this chapter has helped to expand your horizons. For just as God communicated specific guidance during Bible times, he can also do so today. We hope that your expectations have increased that God is always moving in and around us.

During the times of the kings in the Old Testament, Jonathan

knew God didn't need a lot of human power to get a job done. Jonathan teamed up with his armor bearer to assault a garrison of Phil-
istines, "Come, let's go over to the outpost of those uncircumcised
fellows. Perhaps the LORD will act in our behalf. Nothing can hinder the LORD from saving, whether by many or by few" (1 Samuel
14:6). And a youthful David faced down the giant Goliath with
great God-confidence and a sling and some stones:

> You come against me with sword and spear and javelin, but I
> come against you in the name of the LORD Almighty, the God
> of the armies of Israel, whom you have defied. This day the
> LORD will hand you over to me, and I'll strike you down and
> cut off your head. Today I will give the carcasses of the Phi-
> listine army to the birds of the air and the beasts of the earth,
> and the whole world will know that there is a God in Israel. All
> those gathered here will know that it is not by sword or spear
> that the LORD saves; for the battle is the LORD's, and he will
> give all of you into our hands. (1 Samuel 17:45-47)

During the days of Joshua, to cross over the Jordan, the priests
were to lead the way. As their feet touched the Jordan River it would
part and let the whole nation of Israel pass on dry ground, as their
parents had done earlier crossing the Red Sea (Joshua 3:1—4:24).
But the priests had to step out first. Only when their feet ventured
toward the water did the Lord dry up the water. They stood in the
middle of the dry river bed while the nation passed by to the other
side. Joshua ordered one man from each of the twelve tribes to take
out a large stone to be placed on the shore as a memorial to this divine
provision from God. When all had passed to the other side, the priest
then stepped out on the shore, and the waters returned. Likewise, we
must step out to exercise our God-confidence. And it's probably a
good practice to set up memorials to God's provision—perhaps a record in a journal or some simple creative object—to remind us when

we forget or become too discouraged to step out again.

Conclusion

On January 28, 2005, Sophya Salti arrived in this world with a sense of trust that was remarkable, evident even to the nurse standing nearby. Sophya is the first child of Eddie and Donna Salti, good friends from church. During Donna's pregnancy, Eddie would often speak to Sophya in the womb. Over the months of gestation, she came to know his voice, but also his touch. During the later months, Eddie placed his hand on one side of the womb. Sophya would visibly move over to be near his touch. When Eddie removed his hand, Sophya would return to her usual position. The thirty-hour labor was a bit challenging for Donna and Sophya. So, upon her arrival, Sophya was wrapped in a cloth and placed under a heat lamp in the next room. But she cried and cried and cried. Eddie walked over to Sophya, covered her chest and stomach with his hand, and said, "Hey, Sophya, it's your daddy." Immediately, she calmed down, resting under his warm hand and familiar voice. She placed her hands around his, curled her feet up around his hand, opened her eyes and smiled! The nurse noticed how quickly Sophya stopped crying and remarked to Eddie, "You must have talked to her during the pregnancy." At birth, Sophya brought with her an evident level of trust in her dad. That foundational milestone will pave the way for increasing her trust in others, and eventually in God, her heavenly Father.

Whether we came into the world like Sophya or not, our heavenly Abba desires to place his warm hand on us, and let his familiar voice reassure us of his love and compassion for us. For some of us, it will take a bit longer to stop crying, to stop relying on our own limited resources and to respond to God's unconditional love and intimate fellowship. We hope your God-confidence has been increased as you've journeyed through this book, that God has become nearer to you and your expectation has grown.

In the book we emphasized four key themes about God-confidence:

1. Our God-confidence, at its core, is a dynamic, personal relationship with the Triune God: Father, Son and Holy Spirit.

2. Our God-confidence includes our beliefs—our perspectives, our knowledge of reality. Life will involve a series of paradigm shifts as we endeavor to know reality as God knows it.

3. Our God-confidence affects our actions—we were designed by God so that our faith might result in actions. Life will involve a series of practice shifts that correspond to our paradigm shifts. Our lives tend to be governed by, circumscribed by, the current levels of our faith.

4. Our God-confidence—our expectations that God is actively engaged in this world—can grow more and more.

Now it's time to step out and learn more about how God can be trusted. What God-confidence-stretching project comes to mind?

With what earnest zeal and unwearied diligence should
we cultivate [faith]. It is a growing grace. There are no bounds to
its expanse. The more we possess the more we shall gain
and the more we shall realize its power to enter the courts of heaven
and boldly claim communion with our Lord.

HENRY LAW, *FAMILY DEVOTION*

Questions for Personal Application and Group Discussion

1. Look back at some of the good decisions that you've made and ponder the factors surrounding these situations. What specifically contributed to making these good decisions? Likewise, look back at some poor decisions and ponder the factors surrounding

these cases. What contributed to making these unwise decisions? When did you realize it was or it wasn't a good decision? And, in light of the authors' discussion in chapter three about our desires being the place of temptation, what good desires or apparent good was in the background that may have prompted the decision in the first place? From these cases, both wise and unwise, what principles can you take away for future decision making?

2. On page 175, the authors claim that "God is more interested in helping us than we think." What do you think about this statement? In your personal life, do you tend to view God as near and intimately involved with the details of your life, or does he seem distant and far removed from the everyday? Explain your view.

3. The authors described five ways that we can receive God's communication to us regarding personal decision making: (1) by listening to God while meditating on his Word; (2) by inviting others to help us and pray for us; (3) through inner words from God; (4) through inner images, pictures and dreams from God; and (5) through our deepest longings and yearnings. Locate examples in the Bible for each way and examine the particulars in each case. In your journal or small group, reflect on and discuss situations and incidents from your own life in which God has communicated to you through these ways.

4. Take a moment to reflect on an issue or decision you are currently struggling with. List some practical ways you can begin to step out and trust God with this particular circumstance.

ACKNOWLEDGMENTS

Thanks to Gary Deddo, our InterVarsity Press editor, who welcomed the project, offered constructive feedback and helped bring the book to publication. We also are very grateful to Halee Scott for her wonderful work of editing and smoothing out our writing styles to make each chapter more readable. She also developed the discussion questions at the end of each chapter. Of course, we acknowledge the faithful support of our dear wives, Hope Moreland and Beth Issler, for their encouragement, support and help on the book, reading earlier versions of the manuscript.

NOTES

Chapter 1: What Faith Is . . . and What It Isn't

[1]Keith Lockitch, "Reader Rebuttal: Creationism," *The Orange County Register,* December 11, 2005, editorial section, p. 4.

[2]Wayne Grudem, *Systematic Theology* (Grand Rapids: Zondervan, 1994), pp. 710-11.

[3]John Nolland, *The Gospel of Matthew: A Commentary on the Greek Text,* New International Greek Testament Commentary (Grand Rapids: Eerdmans, 2005), p. 716 n. 110, emphasis added.

[4]For more on this, see R. T. Kendall, *Total Forgiveness* (Lake Mary, Fla.: Charisma House, 2002). For an introduction to social science research on forgiveness, particularly the pioneering work of Robert Enright, see Gary Thomas, "The Forgiveness Factor," *Christianity Today,* January 10, 2000, pp. 38-45.

[5]It is interesting to note here that based on research and forty years during which I (J. P.) have spoken on over two hundred college campuses and in hundreds of churches, it is clear to me that atheists regularly have deep-seated, unresolved emotional conflict with their father figures, and it would be foolish to think that this plays no role in their atheism. See Paul C. Vitz, *Faith of the Fatherless: The Psychology of Atheism* (Dallas: Spence, 1999); Benjamin Beit-Hallahmi, "Atheists: A Psychological Profile," in *The Cambridge Companion to Atheism,* ed. Michael Martin (Cambridge: Cambridge University Press, 2007), pp. 300-317.

[6]For more on the hiddenness of God, see J. P. Moreland and Klaus Issler, *The Lost Virtue of Happiness: Discovering the Disciplines of the Good Life* (Colorado Springs: NavPress, 2006), chap. 6.

[7]Francis Fukuyama, "Social Capital," in *Culture Matters: How Values Shape Human Progress,* ed. Lawrence Harrison and Samuel Huntington (New York: Basic

Books, 2000), p. 98. See also Fukuyama's book-length treatment of the subject, *Trust: The Social Virtues and the Creation of Prosperity* (New York: Free Press, 1995).

Chapter 2: Dealing with Doubts

[1]Quoted from Joe Scarborough's interview of Bill Maher on MSNBC's *Scarborough Country,* February 15, 2005.

[2]Dallas Willard, *The Divine Conspiracy: Rediscovering Our Hidden Life in God* (San Francisco: HarperSanFrancisco, 1998), p. 92; cf. pp. 75, 79, 134 and 184-85.

[3]For our purposes, the context and full meaning of each text are not important. What matters is the regular biblical emphasis on having *knowledge* of various things, and not possessing mere belief. The related words in Scripture have been italicized to emphasize this point.

[4]Scott Hafemann, *The God of Promise and the Life of Faith* (Wheaton, Ill.: Crossway, 2001), p. 232 n. 1.

[5]Currently, we are giving a definition of knowledge and not an exposition of how one can tell if one has knowledge in a given case. The former task is one of clarifying what knowledge itself is; the latter of providing a description of the sort of evidence needed to have it. Analogously, it is one thing to define *unicorn* (a one-horned horse) and another thing to cite evidence that would count in favor of unicorns actually existing in Montana (e.g., eyewitness testimony, discovery of unicorn droppings). By way of application, a proper characterization of knowledge in certain cases of religious experience would be an awareness of God's Spirit. It is not our current concern to characterize *accurate* in such a way as to specify the sorts of evidence needed to know a particular case was accurate (e.g., comportment with Scripture, resulting in a specific answer to prayer, contributing to growth in Christlikeness). For more on the characterization of such prayer, see Dallas Willard, *Hearing God: Developing a Conversational Relationship with God* (Downers Grove, Ill.: InterVarsity Press, 1999).

[6]Charles H. Kraft, *Christianity with Power: Your Worldview and Your Experience of the Supernatural* (Eugene, Ore.: Wipf & Stock, 2005), p. 27.

[7]For a discussion of this topic and a bibliography of some of the relevant scientific and philosophical literature, see J. P. Moreland and Scott B. Rae, *Body & Soul: Human Nature & the Crisis in Ethics* (Downers Grove, Ill.: InterVarsity Press, 2000), chap. 6.

[8]Christian Smith, *American Evangelicalism: Embattled and Thriving* (Chicago: University of Chicago Press, 1998), p. 76.

[9]Stephen Carter, *The Culture of Disbelief* (San Francisco: Basic Books, 1993), pp. 4-6.

[10]John G. Gager, *Kingdom and Community: The Social World of Early Christianity* (Englewood Cliffs, N.J.: Prentice-Hall, 1975), pp. 86-87.

[11]Smith, *American Evangelicalism*, p. 156.

[12]Thomas Nagel, *The Last Word* (New York: Oxford University Press, 1997), p. 130.

[13]Douglas Coupland, *Life After God* (New York: Pocket Books, 1994), p. 359.

[14]For more on cultivating the life of the mind in a way relevant to strengthening your faith, see J. P. Moreland, *Love Your God with All Your Mind* (Colorado Springs: NavPress, 1997). For a simplified version of this source aimed at high-school students, see J. P. Moreland and Mark Matlock, *Smart Faith* (Colorado Springs: NavPress, 2005).

Chapter 3: Dealing with the Past

[1]Some names have been changed to protect the identities of certain individuals.

[2]Ed Piorek, *The Father Loves You* (Capetown, South Africa: Vineyard International, 1999), pp. 124-25.

[3]"Getting to Know You," *Family Matters*, Anaheim Vineyard Church, June 2007, pp. 1-2.

[4]T. Sorg, "Heart," in *The New International Dictionary of New Testament Theology*, ed. Colin Brown (Grand Rapids: Zondervan, 1976), 2:181.

[5]Ibid., p. 182.

[6]Bruce K. Waltke, *Finding the Will of God: A Pagan Notion?* (Grand Rapids: Eerdmans, 1995), pp. 86-87.

[7]C. S. Lewis, *The Weight of Glory and Other Addresses* (New York: HarperCollins, 2001), pp. 25-26, emphasis added.

[8]Walter Bauer, William Arndt, F. Wilbur Gringrich and Frederick Danker, *A Greek-English Lexicon of the New Testament*, 2nd ed. (Chicago: University of Chicago Press, 1979), p. 293.

[9]Henri J. M. Nouwen, *The Return of the Prodigal Son: A Story of Homecoming* (New York: Image, 1992), p. 43.

[10]Floyd McClung Jr., *The Father Heart of God* (Eugene, Ore.: Harvest, 1985), pp. 37-38.

[11]Ibid., p. 38.

[12]Scot McKnight, *The Jesus Creed: Loving God, Loving Others* (Brewster, Mass.: Paraclete, 2004), p. 25. Although the Gospels almost always use the Greek term

pater (father) when Jesus speaks or prays, we know that Jesus primarily spoke Aramaic and most likely used the Aramaic term *abba* as he did in the garden (Mark 14:36), the only occasion when a Gospel writer actually quoted his Aramaic usage.

[13]Thomas R. Schreiner, *Romans*, Baker Exegetical Commentary on the New Testament (Grand Rapids: Baker, 1998), 6:426. Schreiner also cautions us against reading too much into the word *abba:* "But some scholars have overplayed the intimacy and uniqueness of the term" (p. 426).

[14]Martin Luther, *A Commentary on St. Paul's Epistle to the Galatians* (London: Clarke, 1953), pp. 369-70; I took the liberty to update the archaic verbs and pronouns in this quotation.

[15]Gerald Wilson, *Psalms Volume 1*, NIV Application Commentary (Grand Rapids: Zondervan, 2002), p. 779.

[16]Ibid.

[17]Translation by Leslie C. Allen, *Psalms 101–150*, Word Biblical Commentary (Nashville: Thomas Nelson, 2002), 21:318.

[18]Henry Cloud and John Townsend, *How People Grow: What the Bible Reveals About Personal Growth* (Grand Rapids: Zondervan, 2001), pp. 254-55.

[19]Charles H. Kraft, *Deep Wounds, Deep Healing: Discovering the Vital Link Between Spiritual Warfare and Inner Healing* (Ventura, Calif.: Regal, 1993), p. 38.

[20]Piorek, *Father Loves You*, p. 68.

[21]Ibid.

[22]Ibid., p. 69.

[23]Ibid.

[24]Clinton E. Arnold, *Three Crucial Questions About Spiritual Warfare* (Grand Rapids: Baker, 1997), pp. 88-89.

[25]Waltke, *Finding the Will of God*, pp. 102-3.

[26]Kraft, *Deep Wounds*, p. 258.

[27]Two independent but related fields of study attempt to clarify the importance of relationships and how they affect our lives. For further study of object relations theory, see Frank Summers, *Object Relations Theory and Psychopathology* (Hillsdale, N.J.: Analytic Press, 1994); for further study of attachment theory, see Steven Rholes and Jeffrey Simpson, eds., *Adult Attachment: Theory, Research, and Clinical Implications* (New York: Guilford, 2004). For a Christian discussion of these theories, see the article by our Biola colleague, Todd Hall, "Psychoanalysis, Attachment, and Spirituality," part 1 and part 2, *Journal of Psychology and Theology* 35, no. 1 (2007): 14-42.

[28]For helpful insights into the dark side of our emotions and our compulsions, see the following resources: David Seamands, *Healing Your Heart of Painful Emotions* (Nashville: W, 2005) [four previous books in one volume]; Kraft, *Deep Wounds;* and Gerald May, *Addiction and Grace: Love and Spirituality in the Healing of Addictions* (San Francisco: HarperSanFrancisco, 1988).

[29]Agnieszka Tennant, "Lives of Quiet Turbulence: Elizabeth Marquardt on What Happens in the Souls of Children of Divorce," *Christianity Today,* March 2006, p. 41.

[30]Ibid. For further information, see Elizabeth Marquardt, *Between Two Worlds: The Inner Lives of Children of Divorce* (New York: Three Rivers, 2005).

[31]Darrell L. Bock, *Luke 9:51–24:53,* Baker Exegetical Commentary on the New Testament (Grand Rapids: Baker, 1996), 36:1062-63.

[32]James Dobson, "Manhood at Its Best," in *The Embrace of a Father: True Stories of Inspiration and Encouragement,* comp. Wayne Holmes (Minneapolis: Bethany House, 2006), p. 18.

[33]Ibid., p. 19.

[34]Ibid., pp. 19-20.

Chapter 4: Making Sense of Jesus' Incredible Promises

[1]Arthur Janov, *The New Primal Scream: Primal Therapy Twenty Years On* (London: Abacus, 1990), p. 310.

[2]For a more detailed study of Jesus and his dependence on God, see Klaus Issler, "Jesus' Example: Prototype of the Dependent and Spirit-Filled Life," in *Jesus in Trinitarian Perspective: An Introductory Christology,* ed. Fred Sanders and Klaus Issler (Nashville: Broadman & Holman, 2007).

[3]D. A. Carson. *Showing the Spirit: A Theological Exposition of 1 Corinthians 12–14* (Grand Rapids: Baker, 1987), pp. 74-75.

[4]Here Christian leaders (e.g., seminary professors, pastors) must be careful not to automatically label beliefs outside their plausibility structures as heresy. The disciples themselves could not believe the women's report that Jesus was alive (Luke 24:11). Christian leaders have a greater accountability as teachers (James 3:1) and must be cautious not to come under Jesus' severe judgment of actually hindering believers from learning more of God's truth because of their own *personal* reluctance to acknowledge God's truth (e.g., Luke 11:52).

Furthermore, why is it that we who talk much about the grace of God sometimes have great difficulty in extending grace to those with whom we disagree? "Dear children, let us not love with words or tongue but with actions and in truth" (1 John 3:18).

[5]Dallas Willard, *The Divine Conspiracy: Rediscovering Our Hidden Life in God* (San Francisco: HarperSanFrancisco, 1998), pp. 75, 77-78.

[6]To explore further how our view of God affects how we live, see Klaus Issler, *Wasting Time with God: A Christian Spirituality of Friendship with God* (Downers Grove, Ill.: InterVarsity Press, 2001).

[7]Willard, *Divine Conspiracy*, p. 61.

[8]Paul Barnett, *The Second Epistle to the Corinthians*, New International Commentary on the New Testament (Grand Rapids: Eerdmans, 1997), p. 250.

[9]George H. Guthrie, *Hebrews*, NIV Application Commentary (Grand Rapids: Zondervan, 1998), p. 375.

[10]George Eldon Ladd, *A Theology of the New Testament* (Grand Rapids: Eerdmans, 1974), p. 630.

[11]Mike Lambly, retold by Gary Kinnaman, "Two Came for Katherine," in *Unsolved Mysteries*, comp. John Van Diest (Sisters, Ore.: Multnomah, 1997), pp. 112-13.

[12]For a brief treatment of the problem of evil, see J. P. Moreland and William Lane Craig, *Philosophical Foundations of a Christian Worldview* (Downers Grove, Ill.: InterVarsity Press, 2003), chap. 27; Issler, *Wasting Time with God*, chap. 7, "Apprenticeship: Yielding to the God Who Disciplines," and chap. 8, "Partnership: Asking the God Who Answers."

[13]For a readable treatment of the categories of Psalms, see Tremper Longman, *How to Read the Psalms* (Downers Grove, Ill.: InterVarsity Press, 1988). For further thoughts on lament, see Michael Card, *A Sacred Sorrow: Reaching Out to God in the Lost Language of Lament* (Colorado Springs: NavPress, 2005). We thank Peter Held for making us aware of this helpful book.

[14]Douglas Moo, *The Letter of James*, Pillar New Testament Commentary (Grand Rapids: Eerdmans, 2000), pp. 238, 243.

[15]R. T. France, *The Gospel of Matthew*, New International Commentary on the New Testament (Grand Rapids: Eerdmans, 2007), p. 279.

[16]For further study of James 4:2 and the concept of impetratory prayer see Klaus Issler, "Divine Providence and Impetratory Prayer: A Review of Issues from Terrance Tiessen's *Providence and Prayer*," *Philosophia Christi* 3, no. 2 (2001): 533-41.

[17]D. A. Carson, *Showing the Spirit: A Theological Exposition of 1 Corinthians 12–14* (Grand Rapids: Baker, 1987), p. 16, emphasis added.

[18]Luke T. Johnson, *Letters to Paul's Delegates: 1 Timothy, 2 Timothy, Titus* (Har-

risburg, Penn.: Trinity, 1996), p. 131, emphasis added.

[19]Thomas Aquinas *Summa theologiae* 3a.7.3 *resp.*, in Gerald O'Collins, *Christology* (Oxford: Oxford University Press, 1995), pp. 254-55.

[20]William L. Lane, *Hebrews 9—13*, Word Biblical Commentary (Dallas: Word, 1991), 47b:412.

[21]Donald Hagner, *Hebrews*, New International Biblical Commentary (Peabody, Mass.: Hendrickson, 1990), 14:212.

[22]Lane, *Hebrews 9—13*, 47b:397.

[23]Harold W. Attridge, *The Epistle to the Hebrews*, Hermeneia (Philadelphia: Fortress, 1989), pp. 357-58.

[24]Sharyn E. Dowd, *Prayer, Power, and the Problem of Suffering: Mark 11:22-25 in the Context of Markan Theology*, Society of Biblical Literature Dissertation Series (Atlanta: Scholars Press, 1986), 105:111.

[25]O'Collins, *Christology*, p. 261.

[26]Ian G. Wallis, *The Faith of Jesus Christ in Early Christian Traditions*, Society for New Testament Studies Monograph Series (Cambridge: Cambridge University Press, 1995), 84:36. Wallis concludes his book with this telling statement: "It is the conviction of the present author that interest in Jesus' faith was an unfortunate and unnecessary casualty of early Christological controversy, in which its significance was determined more in terms of what it conceded to rival positions rather than of what it contributed to our knowledge of God and humanity of Jesus Christ. . . . Certainly, Jesus' faith does seem to provide a point of departure for Christology which is rooted in common human experience and which explores his theological significance through reflection upon his human being in relation to God" (p. 221).

That Jesus expressed God-confidence himself is also supported by a reconsideration of a Greek phrase that Paul uses. The phrase *pistis Christou* (faith of/ in Christ) is used by Paul eight times (Romans 3:22, 26; Galatians 2:16 [twice], 20; 3:22; Ephesians 3:12; Philippians 3:9; it also appears in Acts 3:16 and Revelation 14:12). The issue revolves around whether this phrase should be translated as "faith/trust *in* Christ" (objective genitive) or as "the faith/trust *of* Christ" (subjective genitive). To be clear, this issue does not affect the biblical teaching that believers must place their trust *in* Jesus, as taught in various New Testament passages (e.g., "we have heard of your faith in Christ Jesus," Colossians 1:4; John 3:16; Acts 20:21).

The standard translation has been as "faith/trust in Christ" (objective genitive, e.g., Romans 3:22 [NASB, NIV, RSV, NKJV]). More commentators are recognizing the legitimacy of the phrase as a subjective genitive, that is, "faith/trust *of* Jesus," that Jesus himself experienced God-confidence (see the marginal note in the NIV). Daniel Wallace summarizes the grammatical options in *An Exegetical Syntax of the New Testament* (Grand Rapids: Zondervan, 1996), pp. 115-16. Wallace concludes: "Although the issue is not to be solved via grammar, on balance grammatical considerations seem to be in favor of the subjective gen. view [faith of Christ]" (p. 116). For further study, see Richard B. Hays, *The Faith of Jesus: The Narrative Substructure of Galatians 3:1–4:11,* 2nd ed. (Grand Rapids: Eerdmans, 2001); Morna D. Hooker, *"[Pistis Christou],"* *New Testament Studies* 35 (1989): 321-42; Gerald O'Collins and Daniel Kendall, "The Faith of Jesus," *Theological Studies* 53 (1992): 403-23; and Wallis, *Faith of Jesus Christ.*

So, for example, the apostle Paul expressed his own imitation of Christ's trust in God in Galatians 2:20: "The life I live in the body, *I live by the faith of the Son of God,* who loved me and gave himself for me" (author's translation). George MacDonald, in *Robert Falconer* (London: Hurst and Blackwell, 1868) describes a character, including this idea, "He had ever one anchor of the soul, and he found that it held—the faith of Jesus (I say the faith of Jesus, not his own faith in Jesus)." Cited in *The Wind from the Stars: Through the Year with George MacDonald,* ed. Gordon Reid (London: HarperCollins, 1992), p. 248.

The very posture for how Jesus depended on God, making it possible for Jesus to obey the Father on earth, is how Paul desired to live his life.

[27]D. A. Carson states, "Luke 11:20 has 'the finger of God' instead of 'the Spirit of God.' Possibly the latter is original, . . . but the matter is of little consequence since they both refer to the same thing (cf. Exod 8:19; Deut 9:10; Ps 8:3)." "Matthew," in *The Expositor's Bible Commentary,* ed. Frank E. Gaebelein (Grand Rapids: Zondervan, 1981), 9:289.

[28]G. R. Beasley-Murray, "Jesus and the Spirit," in *Melanges Bibliques en homage au R. P. Beda Rigaux,* ed. A. Deschamps and A. de Halleux (Gembloux: Duculot, 1970), p. 471.

[29]Ibid., p. 471. Donald Hagner agrees: "Given Matthew's christological interests and the unique and central position held by Jesus throughout the Gospel, one may understandably be surprised that Matthew has not said the reverse of what stands in the text, i.e., that blasphemy against the Spirit is forgivable but not that against the Son of Man. The gravity of the blasphemy against the Spirit, however, depends upon the Holy Spirit as the fundamental dynamic that stands behind and makes possible the entire messianic ministry of Jesus itself. . . . The failure to understand Jesus is yet forgivable but not the outright rejection of the

saving power of God through the Spirit exhibited in the direct overthrow of the kingdom of Satan" (*Matthew 1–13*, Word Biblical Commentary [Dallas: Word, 1993], 33a:348).

[30]William L. Lane, *The Gospel According to Mark*, New International Commentary on the New Testament (Grand Rapids: Eerdmans, 1974), pp. 520-21.

[31]E. Earle Ellis, *The Gospel of Luke* (London: Marshall, Morgan & Scott, 1966), p. 85; cf. James 3:15, 17.

[32]Gerald F. Hawthorne draws this conclusion: "Even though Luke does not use the precise words *the Spirit* or *the Holy Spirit* in this particular narrative about Jesus (Luke 2:41-52), there are, nevertheless, sufficient clues embedded in the story to indicate that he surely assumed that his readers would understand that the Holy Spirit in all his power was present in Jesus' life, even when he was a boy of twelve. One may also infer from this account that at every phase of Jesus' life the Spirit was there with him, beside him, upon him, within him to fill him with wisdom and understanding, to guide him in the way of righteousness" (*The Presence and the Power: The Significance of the Holy Spirit in the Life and Ministry of Jesus* [Dallas: Word, 1991], p. 109).

[33]Recognizing that Jesus as a child could walk so closely with the Spirit opens up new possibilities for children, if parents and teachers can show them how to walk with the Spirit.

[34]Experience is one legitimate test for truth about reality, but Scripture is always the primary test (yet we must be humbly aware that our experience can color our interpretation of Scripture; our plausibility structures limit what can be discerned from scriptural data). The classic formulation for the three-factor model of tests for truth includes Scripture, reasoning and experience (e.g., Gordon R. Lewis and Bruce A. Demarest, *Integrative Theology* [Grand Rapids: Zondervan, 1987], 1:8, 150; George P. Fisher, *History of Christian Doctrine* [New York: Scribners, 1896], pp. 10-11). John S. Feinberg (*The Many Faces of Evil* [Grand Rapids: Zondervan, 1994], p. 72) divides the category of experience into two questions: (a) "Does it square with the data of reality so that it is likely to be true, in a correspondence sense of 'true'?" (e.g., 1 Kings 10:6-7; John 20:24-25). (b) "Can one practice such a view on a daily basis?" Another variation, focusing on sources of knowledge, is labeled the Wesleyan Quadrilateral: Scripture, tradition (theology as a human artifact distinct from divine revelation), reason and experience (see Donald A. Thorsen, *The Wesleyan Quadrilateral: Scripture, Tradition, Reason and Experience as a Model of Evangelical Theology* [Grand Rapids: Zondervan, 1990]).

[35]For a biblical defense of God's personal guidance, see Klaus Issler, "Communication: Hearing the God Who Speaks," in *Wasting Time with God*, pp. 151-82; also Dallas Willard, *Hearing God: Developing a Conversational Relationship with God* (Downers Grove, Ill.: InterVarsity Press, 1999). Dallas Willard is one of our credible witnesses.

[36]Charles H. Kraft, *Christianity with Power: Your Worldview and Your Experience of the Supernatural* (Eugene, Ore.: Wipf & Stock, 2005), p. 85, emphasis added.

[37]Michael Atchison, "Mustard Seeds," *The Real Issue* 17, no. 2 (1999): 13.

[38]C. S. Lewis, *Christian Behavior* (New York: Macmillan, 1945), p. 55.

Chapter 5: Bearing Witness to God's Activity in Our World

[1]Christian Smith, *American Evangelicalism: Embattled and Thriving* (Chicago: University of Chicago Press, 1998), pp. 155-60. For two reasons, we will not address the problem of evil and suffering directly. First, the topic has been repeatedly addressed in numerous sources and there is not adequate space to address the problem here. See our brief discussion and related footnotes in the last chapter. Second, the problem of evil is seldom addressed as part of the more general problem of God's apparent inactivity in the world, yet this latter issue is very important, especially in light of our purpose of explaining how to grow in one's confidence in God. We have chosen to address this latter topic with the hope that our exposition will be fruitful in your life.

[2]Ibid., p. 173.

[3]Charles H. Kraft, *Christianity with Power: Your Worldview and Your Experience of the Supernatural* (Eugene, Ore.: Wipf & Stock, 2005), p. 41.

[4]Ibid., pp. 72-75.

[5]Daniel Wallace, "The Uneasy Conscience of a Non-Charismatic Evangelical," in *Who's Afraid of the Holy Spirit? An Investigation into the Ministry of the Spirit of God Today*, ed. Daniel B. Wallace and M. James Sawyer (Dallas: Biblical Studies Press, 2005), pp. 2, 3, 9. For a standard, helpful treatment of 1 Corinthians 12—14, see D. A. Carson, *Showing the Spirit: A Theological Exposition of 1 Corinthians 12–14* (Grand Rapids: Baker, 1987).

[6]Kraft, *Christianity with Power,* pp. 72, 93.

[7]I have taken this story from my book, J. P. Moreland, *Kingdom Triangle: Recover the Christan Mind, Renovate the Soul, Restore the Spirit's Power* (Grand Rapids: Zondervan, 2007), pp. 136-37.

[8]I share more about that difficult journey in chap. 7 of our book *The Lost Virtue of Happiness: Discovering the Disciplines of the Good Life* (Colorado Springs: Nav-

Press, 2006).

[9]James Rutz, *Megashift: Igniting Spiritual Power* (Colorado Springs: Empowerment, 2005), pp. 4-5.

[10]I have taken this story from my book, Moreland, *Kingdom Triangle,* pp. 170-71.

[11]For help in learning to discern God's voice, see Dallas Willard, *Hearing God: Developing a Conversational Relationship with God* (Downers Grove, Ill.: InterVarsity Press, 1999); Jack Deere, *Surprised by the Voice of God* (Grand Rapids: Zondervan, 1996); Mark and Patti Virkler, *Dialogue with God* (Gainesville, Fla.: Bridge-Logos, 1986).

[12]Jim Green, *The Jesus Film Project,* November 2005, p. 1.

[13]Ibid., p. 2.

[14]It is customary to define the natural world as the space-time physical word governed by physical or natural laws. This is the view that is promulgated by those who consider themselves to be naturalists. For more on this, see J. P. Moreland, *Kingdom Triangle,* chap. 2; and J. P. Moreland, *Consciousness and the Existence of God: A Theistic Argument* (London: Routledge, forthcoming). The supernatural world is the (alleged) realm containing angels (good and bad) and God. One purpose in sharing these stories is to build your confidence that the supernatural world so understood is real, so we have followed current usage of *supernatural* to achieve this purpose. In a stricter sense, of course, God is the supreme and only supernatural being (e.g., he alone is the maker of heaven and earth, and he alone has the ultimate authority over all creation).

[15]We briefly touched on this topic in chap. 3. For help in this regard, see Charles H. Kraft, *Defeating Dark Angels: Breaking Demonic Oppression in the Believer's Life* (Ann Arbor, Mich.: Servant, 1992); Clinton E. Arnold, *Three Crucial Questions About Spiritual Warfare* (Grand Rapids: Baker, 1997).

[16]*The Chimes* 64, no. 21 (2006): p. 6.

[17]Holly Pivec, "Exorcizing Our Demons," *Biola Connections* (Winter 2006): 10-17.

[18]Although we were not able to provide an in-depth discussion of these periods in this chapter, we'd like to direct you to some good sources that do discuss this issue, such as Thomas H. Green, *When the Well Runs Dry,* rev. ed. (Notre Dame, Ind.: Ave Maria, 2007); and Klaus Issler, *Wasting Time with God: A Christian Spirituality of Friendship with God* (Downers Grove, Ill.: InterVarsity Press, 2001), chap. 5.

[19]Rutz, *Megashift,* p. 4.

[20]The books in this chapter's endnotes are credible places to start. See also Rich-

ard Casdorph, *Real Miracles* (Gainesville, Fla.: Bridge-Logos, 1976); Mahesh Chavda, *Only Love Can Make a Miracle* (Charlotte, N.C.: Mahesh Chavda, 1990); Reginald Cherry, *Healing Prayer* (Nashville: Thomas Nelson, 1999); Steve and Pam Johnson, *Theresa* (Mukilteo, Wash.: WinePress, 1998); Jane Rumph, *Signs and Wonders in America Today* (Ann Arbor, Mich.: Servant, 2003); John Wimber, *Power Healing* (San Francisco: Harper & Row, 1987).

Chapter 6: Learning to Trust in God for Guidance About Life Decisions

[1]Ken Eldred, *God Is at Work: Transforming People and Nations Through Business* (Ventura, Calif.: Regal, 2005), pp. 21-22.

[2]Ibid., p. 22.

[3]For further study of business and calling, see Wayne Grudem, *Business for the Glory of God: The Bible's Teaching on the Moral Goodness of Business* (Wheaton, Ill.: Crossway, 2003); R. Paul Stevens, *The Other Six Days: Vocation, Work, and Ministry in Biblical Perspective* (Grand Rapids: Eerdmans, 1999); and Scott Rae and Kenman Wong, *Beyond Integrity: A Judeo-Christian Approach to Ethics,* 2nd ed. (Grand Rapids: Zondervan, 2004).

[4]Eldred, *God Is at Work,* p. 22.

[5]Ibid., p. 23.

[6]Ibid., p. 24.

[7]Ibid., p. 28.

[8]Ibid., p. 29.

[9]For example, in *Providence and Prayer* (Downers Grove, Ill.: InterVarsity Press, 2000), Terrance Tiessen presents how Christians would pray differently for some missionaries taken hostage, based on the various major models of providence. For a discussion of this book and the models, see my review, "Divine Providence and Impetratory Prayer: A Review of Issues from Terrance Tiessen's *Providence and Prayer,*" *Philosophia Christi* 3, no. 2 (2001): 533-41.

[10]Gordon R. Lewis and Bruce A. Demarest, *Integrative Theology* (Grand Rapids: Zondervan, 1990), 2:112, emphasis original.

[11]Henry T. Blackaby and Claude V. King, *Experiencing God: How to Live the Full Adventure of Knowing and Doing the Will of God* (Nashville: Broadman & Holman, 1994), p. 76.

[12]Edward Curtis and John Brugaletta, *Discerning the Way of Wisdom: Spirituality in the Wisdom Literature* (Grand Rapids: Kregel, 2004), p. 16. Their book is a very practical study of Proverbs and Ecclesiastes, based on their lifelong study.

[13]Peter Toon, *The Art of Meditating on Scripture* (Grand Rapids: Zondervan, 1993),

p. 73, emphasis added.

[14]Gordon D. Fee, *New Testament Exegesis: A Handbook for Students and Pastors*, rev. ed. (Louisville: Westminster John Knox, 1993), p. 162, emphasis added.

[15]A helpful guide for studying the Bible is Gordon D. Fee and Douglas Stuart's *How to Read the Bible for All Its Worth*, 3rd ed. (Grand Rapids: Zondervan, 2003).

[16]William L. Lane, *Hebrews 1-8*, Word Biblical Commentary (Dallas, Tex.: Word, 1999), 47a:103.

[17]Gerhard Maier, *Biblical Hermeneutics*, trans. Robert W. Yarbrough (Wheaton, Ill.: Crossway, 1994), p. 55.

[18]Michael Casey, *Sacred Reading: The Ancient Art of Lectio Divina* (Liguori, Mo.: Triumph Books, 1996), pp. 63-64. One approach to meditation is praying Scripture passages; see Evan Howard, *Praying the Scriptures: A Field Guide for Your Spiritual Journey* (Downers Grove, Ill.: InterVarsity Press, 1999).

[19]For further study of relationships see J. P. Moreland and Klaus Issler, *The Lost Virtue of Happiness: Discovering the Disciplines of the Good Life* (Colorado Springs: NavPress, 2006), chap. 8; Klaus Issler, *Wasting Time with God: A Christian Spirituality of Friendship with God* (Downers Grove, Ill.: Intervarsity Press, 2001), chap. 2.

[20]See Richard Foster's discussion of corporate guidance in *Celebration of Discipline* (San Francisco: Harper & Row, 1978), pp. 150-62.

[21]See Issler, *Wasting Time with God,* chap. 6, for a biblical treatment of God speaking to believers for personal guidance; see also Sam Storms, *The Beginner's Guide to Spiritual Gifts* (Ann Arbor, Mich.: Servant, 2002); Jack Deere, *The Beginner's Guide to the Gift of Prophecy* (Ann Arbor, Mich.: Servant, 2001).

[22]Bruce K. Waltke, *Finding the Will of God: A Pagan Notion?* (Grand Rapids: Eerdmans, 1995), pp. 86-87.

[23]J. Sidlow Baxter, *Does God Still Guide?* (Grand Rapids: Zondervan, 1968), p. 62.

[24]The story is told by Jack Deere, *Surprised by the Voice of God: How God Speaks Today Through Prophecies, Dreams, and Visions* (Grand Rapids: Zondervan, 1996), pp. 33-36.

[25]John G. Finch, *The Holy Spirit: The Expulsive Power of a New Affection* (Gig Harbor, Wash.: Integration Press, 1997), pp. 29-30.

[26]Jayne Thurber-Smith, "Practice What You Preach," *The WIN-Informer,* November/December 2004, p. 22.

[27]Dr. Ray Pritchard, interviewed by Phil Miglioratti, "Pastors and the Struggle of

Prayer," Crosswalk.com, October 23, 2006 <www.crosswalk.com/1438947>.

[28]Personal communication, November 12, 2007.

[29]For a helpful study of dreams and dreamwork from a Christian perspective, see David Benner, "Dreams, the Unconscious, and the Language of the Soul," in *Care of Souls* (Grand Rapids: Baker, 1998), chap. 8; Morton Kelsey, *God, Dreams and Revelation: A Christian Interpretation of Dreams*, rev. and exp. (Minneapolis: Augsburg, 1991); Morton Kelsey, *Dreams: A Way to Listen to God* (New York: Paulist, 1978); Paul D. Meier, *Windows of the Soul* (Nashville: Thomas Nelson, 1995); and Louis M. Savary, Patricia H. Berne and Strephon K. Williams, *Dreams and Spiritual Growth: A Judeo-Christian Way of Dreamwork* (New York: Paulist, 1984).

[30]Cited in Kelsey, *God, Dreams and Revelation*, pp. 136-37, based on Jerome's Epistle 22 ("To Eustochium"). For additional study see Neil Adkin, "Jerome's Use of Scripture Before and After His Dream," *Illinois Classical Studies* 20 (1995): 183-90; and Neil Adkin, "Some Notes on the Dream of Saint Jerome," *Philologus* 128 (1984): 119-26.

[31]There are ten occurrences of the Hebrew word *anan* in the Old Testament: *Leviticus 19:26; Deuteronomy 18:10,* 14; Judges 9:37; 2 Kings 21:6; *2 Chronicles 33:6;* Isaiah 2:6; 57:3; Jeremiah 27:9; and Micah 5:12. Only three were mistranslated in the Vulgate (those italicized). The other seven occurrences were translated correctly in the Vulgate in various ways (e.g., sorcery, witchcraft, augur, soothsayer). Morton Kelsey, *God, Dreams and Revelation*, pp. 138-39, 284 n. 69.

[32]Donna Gordon Blankinship, "Girl who survived eight days in wrecked car improves," *The Seattle Times*, October 14, 2004 <http://community.seattletimes .nwsource.com/archive/?date=20041014&slug=webhatch147>.

Dreams have prompted some to start business ventures, as reported in Amy Alexander, "IBD's 10 Secrets to Success, Wake Up to Opportunity," *Investor's Business Daily*, July 5, 2005: In 1992 Cynthia McKay launched her home-based gift basket business. Although an attorney by training, she had no business or retail experience. After some time, she was wondering what more the business could be doing and needed some direction. She had a strange dream: she was seated at Starbucks with her drink, "and then I had the idea to franchise the business." She's now chief executive of Le Gourmet Gift Basket Inc., with 410 franchises around the world. In 1994, Caroline MacDougal had a dream. At the time she was employed at The Republic of Tea. In the dream, "I told the president of The Republic of Tea that 'the next product I'm going to create is a caffeine-free cappuccino, and the name of the product is Teeccino.'" After much research and experimentation, MacDougal launched Teeccino Herbal Coffee, which makes an alternative coffee drink, and continues as a successful company.

[33]Waltke, *Finding the Will of God,* pp. 86-87.

[34]C. S. Lewis, *The Weight of Glory and Other Addresses* (New York: HarperCollins, 2001), pp. 25-26, emphasis added.

[35]John Goldingay, *Psalms,* vol. 1, *Psalms 1–41* (Grand Rapids: Baker, 2006), p. 519.

[36]Ibid., p. 520.

[37]For further study on the movements of our heart, see Moreland and Issler, "Forming a Tender, Receptive Heart," in *Lost Virtue,* chap. 3; and Klaus Issler, "The Heart and Spiritual Formation," in *Foundations of Spiritual Formation: A Community Approach,* ed. Paul Petitt (Grand Rapids: Kregel, 2008), chap. 5.

Name and Subject Index

Scripture Index